THE
EMOTION
SOLUTION

THE EMOTION SOLUTION

*Change Your Consciousness,
Change Everything*

FRED CARLISLE

Fred Carlisle Media

Published by Fred Carlisle Media, Cummington, Massachusetts
fredcarlisle.com

Edited and designed by Girl Friday Productions
www.girlfridayproductions.com

Cover design: Paul Barrett
Project management: Katherine Richards
Image credits: cover © Shutterstock/antart

ISBN (paperback): 978-1-7346701-0-3
ISBN (ebook): 978-1-7346701-1-0
LCCN: 2020904536

Dedicated to those who have been judged as too emotional—and to those who aspire to be.

No way of thinking or doing, however ancient,
can be trusted without proof.

—Henry David Thoreau

CONTENTS

AUTHOR'S NOTE

The Emotion Solution is a self-help method to rapidly achieve awareness of higher states of consciousness. Since the discovery of this emotion-driven process is relatively new, and despite its having been used successfully, it has not been studied scientifically; the content herein is for informational purposes only, without any guarantee or assurances. No part of this book should be used as a substitute for professional medical or mental-health therapeutic assessment or treatment. Always seek the advice of your doctor or licensed therapist.

PREFACE

Including All of Yourself in Your Development

This book shows you how to directly access your true nature, the higher self that lies beyond the limitations and dictates of your everyday ego. The arrival of your true self expands your capacity for self-growth and mental well-being to a degree that is difficult to imagine. While this transcendent, healing presence has been the goal of many spiritual teachings, self-realization seekers, creative artists, meditation and mindfulness enthusiasts, and anyone who strives to move beyond the turmoil of a self-absorbed and limited mind, success has often been elusive and long in coming. This no longer need be the case. The emotion-driven, step-by-step Emotion Solution method presented here is easier, more effective, and more reliable, and it can move you deeper into the realms of higher consciousness than any other means of which I am aware. Simultaneously, this method delivers almost any self-development goal with comparative ease. And while the Emotion Solution can be used as a practice in and of itself, it can also serve as an addendum to virtually any self-development practice of your liking, greatly accelerating your progress.

You must be thinking that this sounds too good to be true. Fair enough. But the aim of this book is to demonstrate the veracity of these statements and then provide you with the means to test these statements out for yourself.

Many people assert that we have everything within ourselves that we need to grow and evolve. But we also have a problem. While we might have everything within, we don't allow all parts of ourselves equal input to our growth. In fact, we have been trained to shove vital aspects of ourselves into the deepest corners of our psyche, and by that act, we limit our capability. And the quality we most readily reject is the full range of our emotional nature, a sizable portion of our human energy.

Somewhere in our collective history, we became convinced that the so-called negative or shadow side of our emotional makeup is a bad thing, something to fight and conquer. And this is where much of our evolution stopped, for, as this book will show, when you allow the full extent of your emotional responses to function, you attain the fulfillment that people have historically lacked. It's that simple: pushing away the shadow energies that you *don't* like is exactly what keeps what you *do* want from your grasp. And not only that, you'll see that the rejection of certain emotions is what gives them a dark edge; just by pushing these parts of ourselves aside and carrying on as if we were operating on all cylinders, our now-dissociated energies become free to act out in nefarious ways. Taken in, they teach us and advance our cause; rejected and ignored, they produce the pain and distress we as individuals and society suffer today.

This book shows how to contact the rejected parts of yourself and apply them to your self-development efforts. It enables you to get what you want while also expanding your consciousness into realms without limits. This method requires you to develop a new relationship with your emotions, especially those with which you prefer not to identify, and even those parts that you fear or disown. When you learn to put this technique into practice and make peace with your emotional nature, your growth will spike off the chart. This statement comes from my personal experience, the culmination of a lifetime of experimentation and empirical research, driven by a relentless search for healing and growth techniques that actually work.

From an early age I looked around and knew something was off. Like many young people, I observed the hypocrisy, idiotic sentiment, and nonsensical advice of the adults around me. I was told truths that seemed anything but self-evident, truths that didn't fit me or tally with my experience. My mode of conduct did not mesh with the mode society demanded of me. As a child, I could only hope that what I was told to believe, think, and enact was a joke, a joke that all parents played on their children, and that when I finally came of age, we'd all have a good laugh and start living a real life. This was not to be the case. It would be many years before I emerged from this spurious world.

Along the way I tried just about everything to either fit in or release myself from inner turmoil: immersion in religion, virtue development through refinement of my mind, visualizations, keeping stacks of books on self-healing, therapies, philosophy, and self-improvement. I tried self-erasure, escape, eating my way to happiness and perfection, feeling my way there, feeling my past away, thought control, changing my attitude, altering my beliefs, and more. And I attended workshop after workshop, trained as a gestalt therapist and clinical social worker, studied energy healing, body-oriented techniques, and self-realization—the list goes on. More than a little desperate? Yes. Embarrassing? Definitely. But I didn't care. I would not rest until I found what proved rock solid. I wanted my world to make sense, and I wanted to be content with my lot and know precisely where I fit in.

What I found is amazing. I summoned up, whittled down, and combined the best of what I discovered into a process that creates transformational magic. I've used this process in every avenue of my own life, as well as in my work with others. It never disappoints; it continues to assist, direct, and offer vision to an extent that confounds explanation. All it entails, really, is listening to and finally accepting forgotten parts of the self that beg to be heard. And then something else, some other power, takes over, ushering in what the mind cannot fathom. I believe this process to be nothing less than the way to reclaim our forgotten birthright, our royal road to the realization of what it is to be human. My hope is that this book brings you to the same conclusion.

INTRODUCTION

"Why didn't anyone ever tell me about this?" Matt cried out, nearly jumping out of his seat. I didn't have an answer, although Matt wasn't concerned; he was absorbed in his experience. Because he was an adjudicated youth, probation demanded he undergo anger-management training for an interaction he'd had with a coworker, an interaction violent enough to lead to Matt's incarceration. This also landed him in my social-work office. After initial greetings, we discussed Matt's goals and reviewed his history, including the feelings of powerlessness that gave rise to his anger. We also talked about normal, healthy anger and how letting anger build up contributes to explosively acting it out. Good enough. Now we could get to work.

The first thing I did was entice Matt with a one-dollar wager. I bet him that if he re-created and pumped up the anger he felt toward his coworker, while remaining silent and outwardly immobile, he wouldn't be able to hold on to his anger for long, and it would soon disappear as he entered into a state of nothingness. The challenge engaged Matt's pride. After all, he carried enough rage and anger to land him in a correctional facility; those feelings never seemed that far away, and they certainly seemed dependable enough to bet on. He took the bet.

After coaching Matt on how to mentally reenact the infamous scene in which he'd lost his temper with his coworker, he sat still, closed his eyes, and began intensifying his formidable wrath. His body soon became taut as his rage reached its peak. He kept that posture for an impressive length of time. But then his demeanor softened as his energy began to dissipate and then disappear; he had moved into the predicted state of nothingness. I quietly told Matt to remain still, try to stay with the emptiness, and see what emerged from its depths. After a short time, Matt's eyes bugged open as he cried out. He was now immersed in a transformed state of consciousness. And he was ecstatic. With more coaching, Matt further developed and reveled in his altered state of being, a state that completely compensated for the sense of powerlessness that lay beneath and fueled his anger.

Through the use of a simple technique available to all, Matt had transformed his anger into a deep and profound sense of inner strength and peace, an intrinsic state of being that few are lucky enough to experience. Matt had actually *become* the strength he needed to replace his sense of helplessness. And it was effortless, devoid of any attempt at trying to be something he was not. He had reached this transformative state by welcoming, staying with, and embodying the very emotions that had caused his problem.

Additionally, now that he was freed from the constraints that he normally used to hold his emotional energy at bay, insights into the dynamics surrounding his behavior rushed in. The feelings of helplessness, anger, and outrage that had daunted Matt for so long were suddenly and unexpectedly a nonissue.

This groundbreaking shift of inner landscape had come from within Matt himself. He had activated a fundamental, life-preserving quality that had always been within, a quality that provided his own perfect antidote. And importantly, for the first time, Matt felt a commanding sense of self-agency in changing the predicament that had sidetracked his life. At the end of his session, Matt smiled, handed me a dollar bill, and strutted out the office door.

Matt suffered what we all suffer: trouble and frustration in trying to change for the better. And if you, like Matt, suddenly found that simply inviting the emotional response that you had long avoided is precisely what you needed to overcome what had plagued you, you'd be shocked. And you'd want to know why, after so much futile effort and suffering, this information was so long in coming.

Matt's question about why he'd never been told how to access his innate strength is a good one. While it might provide fodder for conspiracy enthusiasts, the Emotion Solution does not attempt to explain why these methods are not common knowledge. But the Emotion Solution does show you how to gain such access, not only to your inherent power but also to any quality you might need to attain your self-development goals—that is, *any* quality, any internal attribute you need to evolve. And the beauty of the system is that you actually *become* your solution, a solution well beyond anything your mind or ego can produce, for your higher self delivers the gift, fleshed out and complete. This is what the Emotion Solution offers. What you must give in return is a love for truth and a willingness to venture outside the ordinary. If this sounds like a fair exchange, welcome to an epic inner adventure.

CHAPTER ONE

The Road Least Traveled

Your Current Block

One way of looking at our life force is by analogy to a battery: a potential energy source with a positive and a negative pole needed to access its capacities. When the battery's two poles are hooked up to an appropriate task, it can accomplish many a wonder through its now-available energy flow. But take that same battery and hook up only one pole to a task, and it is ineffectual; it can't do anything. Or you can partially block the flow of energy to any one pole and get only partial results.

And this is our problem. By degrees, we suppress one pole of our human life force, and in so doing we get only partial results; we realize only part of our potential. We all do it.

So think of yourself as a battery: your effective output depends upon the degree of energy flowing from one of your poles to the other. The polarities of the human life force are conventionally described as the "positive" masculine pole and the "negative" feminine pole of our nature. For our purposes here, we will follow tradition by focusing on the intellectual and rational qualities of the masculine pole, and the emotional and intuitive nature of the feminine, even though these categories do not always correlate with gender or sexual orientation. If there is a free flow of energy between our two poles, the breadth of our life force is realized. This realized potential can then be applied to any task—in this case, to our work of self-development and fulfillment.

One might assume that common sense would tell us to engage both our poles in equal measure, in order to access our full potential to accomplish our goals. But this is far from the case. We have been taught in Western culture to accept our feel-good emotions and shun our darker emotions, but doing so inhibits a large portion of our energy. The result is a devastating lack of flow between our emotions and intellect. We rarely think about the fact that our darker emotions may prove as beneficial and potentially uplifting as our warm and fuzzy ones; rather, we have been conditioned to fear or reject any emotion that isn't instantly gratifying. We think we can push aside our dark energy, but this is not so, since we inevitably act it out and harm others. This destructive outcome reinforces the indoctrination that says our shadow side brings us to ruin and must be avoided at any cost. But a further price we pay for this dynamic is that, in pushing these emotions away, we actually defeat our attempts at self-improvement. When we fully accept our dark self, it informs, transforms, and propels us forward into the finest realms of consciousness. This virtually unrecognized potential contribution is the missing element that can deliver us from a life spent running in circles, to one in which we pick a destination, navigate, and soar to that destiny.

Energy—For What It's Worth

Emotional energy is just that: energy. Whether the emotion is positive or negative does not really matter. To attain our goals and fully inhabit our humanity, it's critical that we integrate negative emotions along with the positive ones, no matter what our minds may tell us. The magnitude of one energetic pole is dependent on the magnitude of the other, just as the light of day can be recognized only through the dark of night. There's no way around it. Yet we insist on amplifying the positive intellect by diminishing the negative emotion. That doesn't work: our misguided attempt to hold negativity at bay divorces us from the richness, depth, and contrast that life has to offer.

You Can Proceed Only from Where You Are

Another way to look at our problem of attaining our goals is that the only way to reach an objective is to start from exactly where we are. Goal-oriented self-improvement techniques encourage us to become someone other than who we are, beginning from a place other than where we are. That will never work.

Look at the obvious: If you are planning a trip, the common-sense approach is to map your route from your starting point. If your directions tell you to start from a location many miles away, and you then try to start your trip as if you were starting from that distant location, you'll never reach your destination. From your first footstep you'll be lost, with no tangible reference point from which to proceed. Nobody does this. Yet we are told that this is how to reach our self-development goals.

Look at a common ambition. Most people agree that possessing a loving disposition toward another is a good thing, a virtue to be developed, so let's use learning to love someone that you currently can't imagine yourself loving as an example. Implicit in your wish to become loving toward this person is the fact that you presently harbor feelings such as dislike, intolerance, hatred, anger, fear, or, at least, indifference toward this person. In this example we'll use hatred. So say your starting point is one of hatred toward this person, and your goal is to become loving.

While a few techniques might encourage you to consider the fact that you currently hate this person, virtually none will tell you to take a bottom-up approach by starting where you actually are and to fully embody your present state of hatred as your first step toward arriving at your goal of love. This is because most approaches to achieving love favor a top-down, journey's-end view: they tell you that you *should be* loving and that you *should not be* hating, as though you could plant yourself at your goal of love and through this act erase your actual starting point of hatred. Such techniques encourage you to try to be more loving and to act as if you are—to visualize yourself loving this person, to think positively toward this person, to be understanding, to be forgiving, to be compassionate, to give no energy to your hatred or even to deny your hatred, to rethink your faulty thoughts and feelings, and so forth. Because you must start from where you are in order to reach a goal, none of these top-down, destination-first methods work. At times they may seem to work, but not really and not for long.

A lot of emotional energy stands between your hatred and your goal of love—negative emotions that aren't going anywhere until you inhabit them. Energy such as hatred won't change through wishful thinking, for what you hope has changed has the knack of leaking back into the lineup in all its supposed unadulterated glory. But emotional energy does change when you let it run freely through your body to tell you what it will. Then it transforms into another form of energy that never ceases to amaze: the truth of your higher being. If you don't deal with this energy by embodying and transforming it, it will always come back to haunt you, making your efforts at reaching love a sham. But as you'll find through applying the Emotion Solution steps, accepting your present position will always lead you to your goal—in this case a love that you never suspected possible.

To reach a goal, then, such as loving someone you hate, you need to start by fully inhabiting your present negative state. And then, as you continue to recognize and honor all your emotions and your bodily sensations during each successive step of the Emotion Solution, your destination will arrive of its own accord, appearing in a fashion that is always surprising. This book shows you how.

Another reason top-down methods don't work is that there's no conceivable way to tell what the final goal of loving this person will look like, so how can your mind create such a vision to emulate? There are many types and spectrums of love. Maybe you will be anointing this person's feet, or maybe your love will display itself as simply accepting them for who they are while respectfully keeping your distance, knowing that doing otherwise could put you in harm's way. Who knows? You haven't been there. It's ludicrous to say that we should replace our hatred with an unimaginable, unrealized love.

Our True Nature

Try looking at this mind-over-emotions orientation from another angle: we have within us our true nature, a higher, inclusive nature that is part of all creation. Our greatest spiritual and religious leaders, mystics, and masters proclaim this true nature is our deepest reality. But if so, why is this ideal in such contrast to our actual experience? Where does it manifest itself?

To be sure, conditions within our society take us anywhere but to our true nature. We live lives of alienation, want, need, disappointment, opposition, loss, and greed for power and material acquisition, all the while vacillating between the roles of victim and aggressor. Meanwhile, we desperately tell ourselves things aren't so bad, we try to better our lot, and we hope for a finer day. Where is our sense of unity, our sense of wholeness and fulfillment? Our lives might be punctuated with a few such moments when we touch the vastness of our greater selves, yet we don't feel fulfilled for long. An uplifting experience fades away, and we quarrel with our neighbor, grunt in dissatisfaction at our plate of food, trudge off to work in resignation, bemoan our sex life, and fall into depressive states. What happened to our deepest inclusive nature? Why is an abiding sense of satisfaction such an anomaly? To try to compensate, many of us will do almost anything to get in touch with our better selves.

And so you get with a program. How about spending a good portion of your life meditating or praying. Or perhaps if you place yourself in a master's proximity, her holiness will rub off on you; problems solved. Then again, how about acting like that master, giving up everything and devoting yourself to their cause. Or just be in the moment—that's it!

Maybe mindfulness holds the answer. Maybe you need to move your body the right way or ingest the right transformative drug. Make yourself a beacon of compassion and shine your light on and uplift the less evolved. Or banish all thoughts and feelings that contrast to holiness; then you'll arrive. Educate yourself, become creative. While these and other methods might produce some results some of the time, they rarely provide notable transformations. But what if the easiest and most fulfilling approach to realizing our true nature and greater capacities is also the most accessible? And the least accessed? We need only look at what we cast off in our wake.

If we possess a truly inclusive nature that is connected to everything, then it stands to reason that we hold every aspect of that everything within ourselves. How could that not be the case? Everything is everything: us, other, and all else thrown in. By definition, "everything" includes light and dark, positive and negative, good and bad, love and hate, health and pathology, joy and pain, satisfaction and frustration, generosity and greed, life and death, creation and destruction. We are all that and more: Earth, moon, and stars. Simple. The problems arise when we believe that we're composed of anything less. And we ensure that we are less when we reject the emotional energy we find uncomfortable.

Getting rid of painful emotions has long been associated with self-improvement, higher spiritual states of consciousness, and virtuous purity. Our self-development beliefs and practices are fraught with dogma determined to exploit, belittle, or curtail the feminine polarity's disquieting emotions—the justification being our misguided conviction that the more we can ignore, downplay, or even eradicate the bothersome emotions that disturb our tranquility, the more evolved we become. According to such views, pure, thought-based beliefs and ideas aid our development, and bothersome, messy feelings inhibit it. Thinking is favored over feeling, reason and mental inspiration over intuition, dominance over reception and cooperation. We choose the "higher" process promoted by so many traditions—that of generating a persona derived from mental constructs and then attempting to model ourselves after it by ridding ourselves of our so-called emotional baggage, rather than including and accepting the full spectrum of our emotional nature.

But coming up with a vision derived exclusively from our intellect and ego, at the expense of our emotions, is not an effective way to access our true nature or make any other type of self-improvement, any more than amputating a limb leads to the experience of a whole and functioning body. But this is what we do, what we have been taught to do. We have been on a fool's errand: trying to find wholeness by denying a major part of ourselves—our deepest, darkest, feminine, feeling part—while relying on our mind's intellect to fill the gap. This ubiquitous preference for the masculine perspective maintains a schism and an imbalance, both within each individual and within society. It sets us apart from any type of unity. And yet this fragmented viewpoint is popularly considered the basis of advanced practice.

We can be fully human, true to our nature, fulfilled, happy, whole, enlightened, or self-realized only to the degree that we have integrated all aspects of everything that is. And that includes not only our thoughts and inspirations, but the entirety of our emotional energy. The moment we begin to choose what we want or don't want to experience, identify with, or embody, we diminish our contact with that whole; with each instance of selectivity, we grow smaller and smaller and further lose the ability to achieve our goals. We cannot realize our true nature and claim our heritage if we play the part of self-serving little gods and discard the parts of creation that we don't like or that we find inconvenient. Just as the full functioning of society as a whole depends on inclusion, the individual's internal community must include diversity. The more we desire a rich, fulfilling life and consciousness, the more we must allow in.

If we take an honest look at ourselves and those around us, we'll see that affecting a positive, negative-eradicating attitude has offered little, for the undercurrents of our denied selves continue to work away in the shadows. When we let our mind dictate what we should experience and accept, without consulting our embodied-emotional nature and the evolutionary material it provides, we pay the piper; following us as we walk around are our unwanted feelings and emotion-driven thoughts strewn in our wake, and we never notice how they affect others or that we possess less form and substance as a result. Yet we continue to prostitute and exploit our emotional body for our pleasure and kick it aside at the first sign of negativity. Our cast-off and unclaimed negative energy then builds up until it screams out in desperation. And when we can no longer hold an emotion back, we act it out, creating more unwanted emotions that we again do our best to ignore.

But we don't give up. We fight our hated and ignored selves all the more with devices like positive affirmation, training our mind to float by unconcerned, all the while beckoning our bliss. What an achievement (if it could be achieved): peace and compassion pervading our every hour, the joy of following our vision of holiness, a holiness that raises us ever higher above the frays of humanity, where we shine so in hopes that others might aspire to emulate our loftiness. We never consider that we who would shine unconsciously contaminate what we touch. Or perhaps we are pragmatists and employ naked resolve to outright deny and stave off unwanted emotional intrusions, so we can get right down to the business of gratifying our all-pervasive dominant minds. But whether the driving force is practical or spiritual, the end result is self-erasure.

While some people may seem successful at eradicating their emotions, take a close look at them. Their demeanors are often flat and lifeless. These purified thinkers resemble the walking dead. They tacitly disparage what they don't like about the feminine polarity and at the same time promote themselves as "loving and compassionate." Are these the people you really want to imitate? My inclination is to somehow snap them out of it or run in the other direction. Walking into a roomful of such trying-to-be holies is overwhelming; to the emotionally attuned, it is like drowning in the deluge of their denied and discarded hatred, rage, fear, frustration, grief, heartache, and anger at God. Their determined effort to avoid the product of their denied dark side, either by winking at it or by denying that it could ever have been a viable part of themselves in the first place—a holy part, no less—forms the foundation of human suffering.

Negative energy does not just go away. Maintaining a positive attitude that excludes what our ego sees as "negative" creates its polar opposite: a world fraught with and powered by the energy of our rejected life force, whether we realize it or not. Our negative energy desperately needs to be seen, accepted, and loved in order to bring about our finer nature. But we are so wrapped up in our adoration of the positive and aversion to the negative that we rarely consider a different orientation; we are mesmerized into supporting and perpetuating our failed system. A chaotic manifestation rages around us, while those projecting their spiritual bliss are, by omission, the very creators of what they profess to rise so far above.

No greater perversion can be promoted than the idea that the positive half of our nature is superior to the negative half, that the masculine is superior to the feminine, that rational thought and inspiration are superior to emotion and intuition. This orientation stops self-development in its tracks. Sidestep one and you lose the whole. Amid all the talk of unconditional love, the fulfilled realization of our true nature cannot be achieved through bowing down to the masculine while kicking the feminine aside in an overt act of hatred. Those who want to help alleviate personal and societal hardship must first take energetic responsibility by paying attention to their emotional response to a situation, embodying that response, and following the path to their greater self. By gaining this skill, you can resolve past issues, thereby creating a position from which you can see current issues as they actually are—free of tugging, pent-up emotional baggage. You can do this. And with this practice, you'll not only attain your self-development goals, but also realize the biggest blessing of them all: entry into the worlds beyond your ego, where your infinite self resides. These life-changing experiences will all but obliterate the probability of acting out your denied energy.

With continued practice in accepting your darker half, you eventually find that what you formerly considered good or bad loses meaning, and that poles of any nature exist only to push you toward the experience of the whole. What you previously considered negative becomes nothing more than emotional energy forcing its way into the system, seeking acceptance and love, ready to play its part in your evolution. This change in perception might seem heretical to those who trade in emotional control, but if responsibly practiced, it is anything but. Bringing your repressed, denied, and unconscious emotions to the light of day and experiencing them responsibly in loving acceptance will lead to realms of transcendence that methods of control and exclusion can never reach.

The resolution of our divided selves within all spheres of life will not come about by our favoring one polarity over another, but instead by our fully accepting the characteristics of each polarity and working with them as equal partners. Positive and negative poles reside within each of us. This is not a case of men versus women (although it often plays out that way) or positive versus negative, for all of us hold traits that are both masculine and feminine, positive and negative, regardless of gender. Harmonizing our individual inner polarities is what will move us beyond where we've been stranded for so long. But while balance between the poles is required, the so-called negative, feminine polarity has been subjected to far greater degradation than the masculine, positive polarity and therefore now needs more attention. This calls for a temporary shift in bias; we need to devote extra care and encouragement to our emotions until they attain their rightful position. And then when our emotions and intellect begin to work in harmony, we'll know that it is time to balance this bias. The ideal is equivalence and cooperation, for these conditions result in stellar evolution and the fulfillment of the heart's desires.

Once you personally experience previously avoided emotions, you won't question the power that they make available. Life's context and priorities change, transformed by foundational changes in consciousness itself. If you want to become more or better, or just outright evolve, this is your path. Nothing gets you there faster. And nothing gets you there with more of yourself intact, enabling you to go far beyond what you thought possible. Your mind doesn't know about this process, for if it did, you would already be using it. But your emotions are ready and waiting to take you there right now, if you give them the chance.

This book proposes that any shunned emotion, in any particular moment, is exactly what you need at that moment to grow and thrive, and that the best way to realize your self-development potential is to accept and embody that emotion without reservation. You don't have to wait to apply this approach to your self-development work. In fact, if you do, you are wasting a golden opportunity to attain your desires. Your emotions are there right now—and if you haven't noticed, they will return to haunt you again and again until you listen. When you finally pay attention to and responsibly embody their energy, they will take you not only to your goals, but also to horizons unforeseen. Always. This is the missing factor of self-development programs: nothing more than admitting into your growth the seemingly rogue elements that you have been taught to discourage. The irony is that the moment you let these elements in is when the party finally begins.

CHAPTER TWO

Before You Begin

As I have argued, casting aside your emotions cuts you off from the self-improvements that you desperately seek. What you feel impelled to change, suppress, repress, and otherwise avoid are the forces that actually hold the answers to the problem of separation from your whole self. If you lovingly accept those emotions and allow them to evolve in balance with your reason, the deepest reaches of your emotional nature will lead you, without fail, to your true self and to levels of sweeping change that must be experienced to be believed. For now, though, you can assume that you are far from being able to accept all of your emotional energy and that you possess a backlog of rejected and unprocessed material. And because the power of these emotions has built up a charge, a charge that is hungry for liberation, you must take certain precautions when releasing your pent-up emotional energy.

Find a Safe Location

Your first precaution is finding a private, safe place in which to do your explorative work, a place where you won't be interrupted or interrupt others. You may well be making noise, so consider the fact that sound travels. If you must engage in this process where someone is within earshot, you can make louder noises into a towel or pillow to muffle the sound and remain private. If your emotions get triggered in public, try to wait until you are in a private place to process them. If you're concerned that your feelings will go away before you have the opportunity to work with them, don't be; the emotional trigger and consequent charge aren't going anywhere. Reexperiencing the event later should not be a problem.

Accept Emotions, Don't Act Them Out

This work is about taking responsibility for and ownership of your emotions. It leaves no room for acting out and hurting another person, either physically or emotionally. You might spew emotions at or in the presence of someone else by accident, yet accident or not, this is not responsible behavior. Experience will teach you how and when and what to safely process in the presence of others, but until then you should attend to reactive material in private or in the presence of a trusted confidant who knows and agrees with what you're doing. If, while in your private location, you need to reenact a situation that includes expressing and exploring disturbing emotions that you harbor toward another person, congratulations—you are finally working toward resolving an issue you've probably been carrying for some time and would otherwise continue to carry. Expressing and taking ownership of dark emotions in private is not being hurtful; it's being responsible. Accepting emotions so that you can transform them, rather than leaving victims in your wake because you act out your unwanted emotions, is the cornerstone of the Emotion Solution.

Always use caution when exposing emotionally driven material, especially if it has been pent up. While learning the process of opening to the denied self, there is no guarantee that long-denied emotions won't suddenly pop up and find expression in the wrong place. But keep in mind that before now, even if you were careful, you acted out your unattended, denied, and repressed emotions, thereby guaranteeing havoc for yourself and others. Now you are working to end this behavior. So open up to your emotions in a safe environment. Also, begin with less intense material and then move deeper only when you are ready. When you take these precautions, the rewards far outweigh the risks. And with a little experience, processing emotions naturally gets easier, for as you begin integrating your estranged energy, you reclaim parts of your innate self, and your added breadth acts as a stabilizing force for further progress.

Avoid the Self-Rejection Trap

In the years of experimentation required to come up with this system, I made plenty of mistakes. The worst had to do with acting out my self-hatred, something we all possess. I wanted to find solutions to resolve my emotional pain and improve my lot. I tried most everything. Eventually reason and intuition told me that freedom from my emotional pain would come through exploring and coming to terms with its origins, and so this is where I focused my efforts. Before long, I learned about and began experiencing relief through catharsis. This emotional purging felt so liberating that I was sure I'd found my answer. Wanting to investigate catharsis to its limit, I employed an experienced professional, and together we aggressively deconstructed my defenses, leading to more emotional venting and more and more cathartic release. At the time, I did not realize that I was actually attacking myself, prompted and powered by a deep-seated self-hatred. Let me explain.

We all possess self-hatred, some of us more than others, but hatred toward our darker, emotional self is something we all share. Take a moment right now and simply look at the judgments and subsequent restraints you place on your emotions and their expression, compared to the extent to which you allow and rely upon the free flow of your intellect. The difference is obvious. When I began bathing in cathartic expression, I didn't realize that I was actually trying to get rid of my emotions as a means to improving myself; I was trying to destroy a necessary part of myself through a pronounced and effective act of hatred and revenge directed at my emotional nature. Being pretty good at detecting and laying bare my defenses in order to reach emotional catharsis, I relentlessly tore myself apart. This did not end well. It took me years to reconsolidate my fractured self to the point at which I could once again make forward strides. Although my case of acting out of emotional self-hatred was extreme, we all do it to some extent. Disregard for your emotional body can range from the overt to the insidious and almost imperceptible, and yet it is always self-destructive, no matter its intensity or depth.

Those who discover the benefits of exploring and releasing bottled up emotions often tackle the challenge with a vengeance, and doing so with the Emotion Solution is particularly tempting. This is because the method not only offers relief by releasing emotions, but it also radically and favorably alters one's experience of self and life through spiritual experiences and higher consciousness. So, of course, people want more of these benefits, and they want them as quickly as possible.

The problem comes when you interpret the Emotion Solution solely as a way to become more positive, spiritual, and healed, despite your emotions. When you don't actually accept negative emotions but rather hope to get rid of them, you may reach a higher state of being, but you can't stay there for any length of time. You might think that by denying your negative emotions you are acting in a loving way, but you aren't. Your emotional body possesses a consciousness of its own, and it will not tolerate your prostituting what you consider its negative aspects as a means to gain access to what you consider positive. Such veiled hatred toward your feminine emotions guarantees the disappearance of a fully functioning emotional body. Wanting an emotion to change to satisfy your narcissistic needs is a dead end, while accepting and loving an emotion opens the door to the greater you.

This distinction between rejection and acceptance cannot be overstated. Picking up on rejection can be easy at times, but more often it is nuanced and difficult to discern. Wanting to rid yourself of an emotion means wanting that emotion, that part of you, not to exist, and acting on this desire, consciously or not, is self-destructive and self-diminishing. Conversely, accepting an emotion means wanting that emotion to thrive as it is, painful or not, and this self-loving act leads to an ever greater sense of self and presence.

I have found that the safest tactic is to assume that your best intentions may not be as benevolent as you might think. Rejecting emotional input is an ingrained habit, one that is difficult to break. Even when you become aware of your tendency to do it and you guard against it, wily self-justification, knee-jerk rejections, and plain habit can slip in and dictate an adverse course. If you don't maintain constant vigilance in seeking out and working through your tainted attitudes, your emotional self-hatred will assume command of your self-development work, and the subsequent repercussions will slow down, if not stop, your progress.

Don't Force It

Similar problems occur when people try to force themselves to feel emotion. Ideally, your emotional evolution is a natural, progressive process. While some methods promote ways of gaining access to material that are relatively safe, others can dredge it up before you have the capacity to process it. Emotions, like onions, have concentric layers that must be peeled back from the outermost to the inner; the presence-of-being gained from processing emotions closer to the surface is needed to safely reveal and integrate those on a deeper level. Otherwise disorder and instability reign. It is a matter of self-protection not to go too deep, too fast. Follow your actual present state in a kindly manner. If you don't push yourself to be where you *think* you should be, you'll reduce the risk of complications.

In all instances, listen to yourself. As your new relationship with your emotions progresses, your intuition, intellect, body, and heart will be ever more able to inform you when you are acting in opposition to your sense of integrity.

CHAPTER THREE

Overview of the Steps for
Following Your Emotions

If you've read to this point and observed that you've failed to make substantial gains in self-development and that your mind tends to exclude much of your feeling nature, and if you're considering connecting with your shadow self as a solution, then good—you probably realize that you want to give it a try and begin by taking the precautions outlined above. So here is an overview of the Emotion Solution process. It is composed of five successive steps—although in practice, these steps can move back and forth, blend, or change position:

1. Recognize
2. Express, Explore, Embody
3. Internalize
4. Transform
5. Unify Through Time

Recognize

The first step of the Emotion Solution is to recognize the emotion and accompanying bodily felt-sense that surface in reaction to your not achieving a self-improvement goal or in reaction to an event in your life. Such reactions are likely to be exactly what you're trying to ignore, overshadow, or eradicate. Recognizing what is actually taking place, rather than what you'd prefer, is often the most difficult part of the Emotion Solution process, but it is a necessary first step.

Express, Explore, Embody

Now that you've identified your reactions, it's time to outwardly express your thoughts and feelings through sound and body and allow them to take you where they will.

If you don't fully participate in this step, your experience will remain lifeless and disembodied, and you will restrict any potential strides forward, but fully engaging will allow your previously shunted energy to take hold and come alive down to the level of your very cells. During this process, you will likely delve into your history, make connections and discoveries, and move in unexpected directions.

Internalize

When your outward expression has concluded, you will need to regenerate that same emotional energy but maintain it internally.

Transform

Transformation occurs through its own volition and seems to come from nowhere, although many call it a gift from a greater self or from God. However you view its appearance, your only role in the transformation is to set up the conditions conducive to its appearance, watch for its arrival, and let it grow and expand your perception. Along with providing a perfectly tailored state of being to resolve your self-development problem, transformation is usually accompanied by far-reaching insights.

Unify Through Time

Unlike transformation, unification is a conscious act. You've reached this step if you have achieved transformation and worked through and made the connections between a past issue and your present difficulty in reaching a self-development goal or resolving a life problem. The unification process informs your brain's emotional centers that the issue is resolved, thereby ensuring that your symptom will not reappear.

Further explanation of these steps in the following chapters will help you achieve the gift that, through the Emotion Solution, you can give yourself.

CHAPTER FOUR

Step 1: Recognize

The first step of the Emotion Solution is to recognize the problem—to identify it and its emotional content, and to acknowledge that it hampers your self-development practice or impedes your day-to-day life. While often a problem and its emotional content are all too apparent, just as often the components evade explicit identification. Many forms of self-improvement work ask us to ignore or somehow override the stumbling blocks and contrary impulses that appear in our life. Or some tell us to notice what passes through our consciousness, put it aside, and carry on. And then some techniques encourage us to investigate emotion-charged problems as a natural part of ourselves, something worthy of our attention. The Emotion Solution carries this last option to a conclusion that is rarely imagined. So in this first step, your goal is simply to recognize the contrary thoughts, feelings, and behaviors that you experience when merely thinking about a problem in your self-improvement practice or life, or one that crops up when you actively try to improve yourself.

At first you are bound to see red flags. They can be as simple as your dislike of self-development work, your resentment of the time-to-results ratio, or your frustration with your lack of overall progress in overcoming an inner conflict; or they can be as obvious as your dissatisfaction with your teacher (if you are enrolled in a formal program). Later on, as you resolve the apparent obstacles and develop your self-examination skills, you'll begin to uncover obscure, subtle reactions and deep-seated beliefs that undermine your efforts. But because of our societal conditioning, even some of the more pronounced impediments can be difficult to perceive. And what clouds self-perception most of all is our tendency to prefer to maintain positivity.

Cultivating pleasant thoughts and harnessing pleasure dominate so much of our day-to-day behavior that we have become incompetent at identifying information that might suggest something other than pleasure. Add to this factor that we're taught negative emotions have nothing to offer but hardship, and you can see the problem. Little considered is the idea that dark emotions can lead straight to your true self and that the failure to give them their due squanders your opportunity to grow. Yet no degree of positivity can override a negative emotion forever. You'll be left with the deleterious effects of your avoidance infiltrating your disposition, typically sunny or not.

You need perseverance to overwrite automatic impulses toward positivity and other misguided behaviors that pull you away from dealing with your darker self. Recognizing the problem is the first, critical step in allowing uncomfortable emotions and emotion-driven thoughts to flourish and lead you to transformation. And there is no better time to acknowledge the fact than the present moment.

Recognizing Existing Contrary Attitudes

For the purposes of this chapter, I am going to use as an example a mixed attitude toward your self-development work, one that creates a barrier to reaching your goal. We will accomplish this elucidation by using the gestalt chair technique. Keep in mind that this procedure can bring you well beyond the Recognize step and into the conclusion of the Express, Explore, Embody step. But here we'll take as our primary goal the simple recognition of the problem. If you find the chair technique useful, any additional material you pick up while you're using it can be carried forward into the following steps.

The Exercise

This exercise can be used to look at your relationship with your self-development work, whatever that might be. Perhaps you are involved in a structured program to better yourself and you are dissatisfied with your progress; or you're simply trying to be a better person; or you want to resolve a day-to-day inner conflict. Perhaps you just want to get through each day intact, and you are using your usual methods for doing so. It makes little difference. You know what you're doing to improve your lot, and there is a good chance your attitude toward your efforts and your results is ambivalent. In this light, we will use the chair technique to temporarily divide you into two parts or selves: a part of self that supports your usual efforts at self-development and a part that does not. While you may already recognize your conflicting selves and find them familiar, this exercise should add new dimensions to your understanding.

To set up the exercise, take two chairs and place them facing each other, a few feet apart. These chairs will be the seats for your opposing parts: when you sit in the first one, you are the part of you that approves of your self-development work—we'll call it the pro-practice self. When you sit in the second chair, you are the part of you that does not approve of or is disenchanted with your self-improvement efforts. We will call this your contra-practice self. Now you will initiate a conversation between your two selves.

Start in the pro-practice chair. Let's say that you want to become fit. Staying in the present tense, tell the (now empty) contra-practice chair all about the benefits of applying yourself to your fitness regimen. You can include everything you've been told to believe works, along with the benefits you've discovered for yourself. It is important to stay in the present moment, speak in the present tense, and make it real. Elaborate. Gush, if that feels right. Get a good felt-sense of yourself in your pro-practice stance. How does it feel to inhabit this chair? You might feel righteous, self-assured, unsure of yourself, or maybe even silly. If so, say so. How do you feel in your body? Whatever comes up is fair game. When you feel that you have made your point, move into the contra-practice chair.

The Contra-Practice Position

Take a little time to sink into the contra-practice position. This self has now heard about the positive aspects of your practice, and it's time to give your pro-practice self your (contra-self) reaction. Inhabiting this perspective can be difficult at first—this may be a part of you that you prefer to avoid—but you can trust that there is material here. Take your time and notice. Again, speak in the present tense. Explain that you heard what your pro-practice position had to say, but that's only one side of it. Begin by informing your pro-practice self about your reservations. Pay particular attention to the emotional content and bodily sensations that come up. Keep in mind that this position can take one of many faces. Maybe you consider your pro-practice self (and fitness program) a failure. Maybe just thinking about that "positive self" makes you fidgety and confused, and you want it to go away, or you're frustrated with it for not gaining enough ground. Maybe you fear that you won't ever get it, that change is impossible for you. Or maybe you just don't want to hear the goody-goody version from your pro-practice self.

Whatever the elements of your opposition, explain to your pro-practice self how what you heard it say might not be completely true, how your fitness practice may not be working all that well for you, or whatever comes up that applies. Encourage these reactions.

Arguments and overt indignation are common in this scenario. As always, pay particular attention to your body's felt-sense, often the truest indicator of what's cropping up. What is your primary emotion? Take your time, and watch for nuance if the process snags or slows down. When you feel you have no more to say, move back to the pro-practice chair, settle in, and respond to your contra-practice self. Continue the conversation, alternating chairs.

When this conversation has served its purpose of recognizing the problem, its primary emotional content, and the felt-sense of your contra-practice self, you can move on to the next step (which may include further working the chair technique). But if you still cannot identify a problem, you can try the chair routine again from its inception.

An alternative to the chair technique is to enter into your regular practice routine and notice interfering reactions, inner thoughts, feelings, sensations—something you've been keeping in the shadows but are now willing to bring to light and consideration. Find the primary emotional content and felt-sense at play, and then proceed to the next step.

Learning to recognize your inner activity requires increasingly subtle perception as you move into deeper structures. But subtle or not, this avoided material is exactly what will lead to the changes you seek and to ever greater depths of self and humanity. And once you begin experiencing these benefits, you'll find that feigning a positive disposition loses its appeal, and you'll place it on the shelf along with other toxic substances. It is a waste of time and effort and has little to do with realizing your true self.

CHAPTER FIVE

Step 2: Express, Explore, Embody

In this step, you'll expand your identified emotion by expressing it through your voice and your body, and by following that thread, you will let its energy take you where it will. You're giving your emotions an actual voice, one that comes from your body, and you're learning from the experience. In our present-day culture this is not considered a natural process, but it should be.

To make this step easier, we'll first approach the work through a different perspective. Then we'll consider the need to move beyond judgments, the problems created by favoring one emotion over another, and the role of catharsis in this system. Finally, before moving into the Express, Explore, Embody procedure itself, we'll discuss setting a tone conducive to your success. You can find additional perspectives, suggestions, and tips for effective processing in chapters 10 and 11.

A Different Perspective

This work isn't about letting your dark side take over. Actually, your darker self already has a seat at the helm, for to the degree that you push dark emotions aside, you let them direct you with a will of their own. So rather than encouraging your emotions to act out in the dark by tacit omission, shine a light on your darker energies. By letting them be simply what they are, you are permitting them their rightful place in your psyche, thereby contributing to your wholeness.

Try looking at it from another viewpoint: you are learning to love what you hate, or learning to embrace what you don't love. The irony is that when you learn to accept and love what you hate (love your enemies)—and that doesn't mean acting out, but responsibly allowing the energy to flow within you—your capacity to love increases dramatically without further effort. Another depth of irony is that our society and its institutions, including our spiritual institutions, ostensibly subscribe to the hatred of dark emotions as the antidote to strife and the path toward love. The antithetical advice presented here—to embrace long-repulsed emotions—may sound far-fetched or sacrilegious, but the act of consciously inviting such emotions in will soon prove otherwise. You are taking responsibility for ignored yet powerful and productive parts of yourself and explicitly making them your own. When you take them in as they are, they will not let you down. Opening up toward your unwanted emotions offers rewards that rejecting them (under the guise of love) cannot. Eventually this perspective will become self-evident, but if it is not obvious now, simply entertain the possibility that it may be valid. Such temporary changes in perception can expedite the questioning of long-held assumptions that inhibit emotional movement.

Judgments

We judge many parts of ourselves as unacceptable and thus hold these parts at bay. Or we project what we cannot accept about ourselves onto others and society. Either way, judgments choke your progress by labeling much of your and others' experience as invalid. In this way, judgments make it impossible to explore all the factors that might determine your truth. Gaining distance from inhibiting judgments of your own emotions and of emotional processing is essential in allowing a fresh perspective from your higher self. Let's discuss two methods that can help you move past process-inhibiting judgments.

The first technique is to sever (at least temporarily) the tie between you and your judgment. Let's say that you judge yourself unworthy of having good things in your life, but simultaneously you want to have good experiences. Your self-judgment as unworthy will pretty much block that progress from happening. A solution to get past this self-limiting judgment is to say out loud, "I renounce my judgment that I don't deserve good things in my life; I no longer believe this to be true. I hereby invite good things and events into my life." Or something along these lines. If you like, you can go into the details of why your judgment is wrong: that it is destroying your chance at success in life, that you're tired of being under its thumb, and so forth. However you word it, this must be a sincere, heartfelt, emotion-charged declaration. Holding your judgment in abeyance creates the opening that allows you to express, explore, and embody.

Another useful and lasting way to defuse a judgment is to work directly with its emotional charge. This method presupposes that you are relatively comfortable with processing emotions, so it does not work with a judgment that condemns emotional work in general. Let's go with the example of your not believing that you deserve good things in life. Insert your sense of unworthiness into the Emotion Solution process. If you decide to employ the gestalt chair technique, you become an undeserving self in one chair and a self that deserves good things in the other chair.

After you recognize your internal dynamics, continue through the remaining steps. If successful, you will come out at the other end with an unexpected sense of self-worth, making your identification as "unworthy" powerless, if not outright silly.

Your Fallback Emotion

We've covered positivity and its detrimental effects. Favoring one emotion over another leads to similar setbacks. Have you ever been hurt, and instead of experiencing the pain involved, you resorted to anger? Perhaps, in general, you feel more comfortable expressing aggression than exposing your vulnerability. Or maybe anger frightens you, or you view it as something so far removed from your identity that you display sorrow or fear when anger is more appropriate. A major problem with such preferred responses is that you cannot substitute an emotion that you accept for one you avoid and expect to resolve your issue. Most people unknowingly resort to this behavior, and it can be difficult to detect. But start to take notice. If you find yourself repeatedly responding to different types of circumstances with the same emotion, you can assume that another unexplored emotion is at play and must be addressed. Simply suspecting that you may tend to override one emotion with another helps avert this dynamic.

Catharsis

The work of the Express, Explore, Embody step often includes catharsis, when strong or repressed emotions seem to take off on their own, and relief arrives through finally venting them. Although you may find relief through catharsis, this is not the final goal of the Emotion Solution process, for alleviating emotional pressure is meager fare compared to what you can achieve by going further. In this work, catharsis can be seen as a particularly clear example of the culmination of the Express, Explore, and Embody step, but keep in mind that it is only one signpost of change that leads to the final settlement of an issue. In other systems, where catharsis is used as an end unto itself, your emotions' origins and triggers usually remain intact, and the cathartic experience must be repeated again and again in order to provide subsequent relief. Add to this the fact that cathartic repetitions can be damaging in themselves, reinforcing the effects of the original trauma.

In the Emotion Solution process, potentially damaging repetitions and overexposure to catharsis are not necessary, for an issue that's been further resolved through transformation can no longer have a place in your changed consciousness. You can certainly welcome catharsis, but stopping at this signpost would not serve your higher learning.

Setting the Stage

Before beginning explorative work, voice your intention for the session out loud. Say, for instance, that your objective is to be able to forgive someone you currently resent. The usual prescription for finding forgiveness is to forget the original offense and replace your resentment with something closer to love. The assumption of the Emotion Solution is that if you explore and fully follow and experience the resentment itself, forgiveness will occur on its own—a pure state of forgiveness that comes from your higher nature and requires no further effort. So because your intent in the Emotion Solution process is to explore your resentment in order to find forgiveness, say it out loud: "My intent at this time is to explore my resentment toward _____, so that I may better understand my motives and find forgiveness." You cannot predict how this forgiveness will play out, but such a statement will objectify and make clear your intent to heal the rift.

Or perhaps you practice meditation and have become frustrated with the process. You might say, "My intent is to fully experience the frustration I encounter while meditating, so that I can learn from my frustration and become more present while meditating." Good enough. You've set the stage for the process at hand.

Some people also ask for guidance and/or protection while working with long-held emotional material. Now would be the time to do so. As with voicing your intent, stating your request out loud seems most effective. Some look at this as a form of prayer, while others frame it as connecting to their higher self or spiritual guide. Understanding how or why requesting assistance is effective is not as important as finding an invocation that works for you.

Express, Explore, Embody

What follows are ideas for inviting, opening up to, and moving through emotional material. While the results of the process of unfoldment are generally predictable, the path can be anything but. We meet up with the unexpected and take surprising detours that can turn a planned sequence upside down and around. And keep in mind that the particulars of the emotional content and all that surrounds it are rarely what you expect, as often these elements seem to come from nowhere and morph on their own. Uncertainty in any given moment is common, as is the need for creativity. From this standpoint, the following is meant as a suggestion rather than as a definitive road map.

Fashion the process to meet your individual needs and your changing situation.

Begin Your Exploration

You can now begin to express, explore, and embody—assuming that you are in a safe location, have stated your intent, have requested guidance and protection, know the difference between processing emotions responsibly and acting them out, and remember not to force emotions but to work with those closest to the surface.

The idea is to pull out the stops on what you have recognized in the previous step. At times you will move your emotions to the point at which they take on a life of their own, leading you through your past, to where you will make insights and connections. At other times such depth is unnecessary. With time, you will get a handle on what is needed in a particular situation; plus you will always be able to tell from a lack of results in the Transform step if you need to deepen your exploratory work.

In any case the roots of many self-development blocks can be traced back to your early history, so in large part, you will be following your emotional content, thoughts, and intuition back to historical events and experiencing that past pain and hardship as if they were occurring in the present moment. Previously, you never allowed yourself or had the capacity to digest this material; it was scary, and you hadn't been taught how to attend to it. But now, as an adult, you are teaching and allowing yourself to process historical experience and move on.

Getting into Emotions

The contrary reaction that you recognized in the first step of the Emotion Solution serves as your jumping-off point. Remember, don't force anything; overriding or leaping past your boundaries and capability always proves unproductive. At the same time, let your energy move. Let yourself go. This is about expressing, exploring, embodying—coming to whole-heartedly own and inhabit this part of yourself. If you like, go back to the gestalt chair technique and really have a go at it. Often it can carry you through to the conclusion of this step. In any event, now is the time to express.

Use sound. This is your emotions' turn to speak, so give them voice. Words may come up, and that's fine, but producing pure sounds often develops emotional content more efficiently. Moreover, pure sounds keep you out of your head; emotions expressed as sound allow you to move into uncharted territory, whereas the structures and meanings that are held in place by thoughts and words will not. Making wordless sounds is especially useful for accessing preverbal material from early childhood. And sound coupled with movement is especially effective in adding dimension and vibrancy to your work.

Producing sounds that represent your emotional state sometimes comes easily and sometimes does not. If sounds don't come up on their own, don't worry. Start to emit any sound that comes to mind, repeat it, and let it change and develop as it will until it becomes genuine. Or it may be easier for you to begin by expressing emotions with words and letting those words evolve into the wordless sounds that can lead you further in. Pure sounds can, and often do, morph several times in the course of a session; they can range from loud, to soft and pleasing, to guttural and animalistic, propelling you through the explorative process. Taken to its conclusion, sound can lead to emotions, insights, and revelation that can be difficult to access otherwise.

At the same time, embody. Pay attention to physical sensations, small and large, for they often present clues to deeper truths. Move in response to the emotions involved, if that seems appropriate. Since emotions respond to and express themselves through your body, you may tense up, shake, writhe and flail, jump around, or crumble lifelessly. Whatever. Just go with what comes up and move as deeply as you feel comfortable doing. If movement doesn't initially happen on its own, once again you can intentionally induce action, such as the classic hitting a pillow if you suspect anger. Add sounds. Before long, your acting will induce the free flow of authentic anger.

Body movement brings about and enhances expression. It also keeps you out of your head, leaving room for other sources of input. Another good trick for staying out of your head is keeping part of your awareness on your arms and legs. This technique is simple and effective. Movement, sound, and simply paying attention to your body during the process will ground you and will bring your emotions home, into your cells, and to life.

All the while, explore. Exploration takes place through thought flashes and intuitive leads and insights, augmented by your willingness and interest and the amount of attention and freedom you give to moving in your emotion-guided direction. It may include images, colors, smells, or felt experiences, like the sensation of being stuck or floating in endless space. Pay attention and investigate. Take whatever comes up, wherever it goes. Exploration becomes increasingly efficient and accurate with practice.

Again, this isn't a linear process. It takes some doing. You may move from one emotion to another or have insights that take you further in or back and forth into your history. Follow your evolving emotions, sensations, and perceptions. At times you'll need to work through layers. Perhaps you're working with anger toward your practice or teacher, and you reach a dead end. Eventually you realize that you cannot process your anger because you're afraid of it. Since it's impossible to welcome a feared emotion, and overriding one emotion that's overshadowed by another never produces favorable results, processing your fear first is key. Once you've accomplished this, you should be able to work through your anger with relative ease. Encountering layers is commonplace.

So cry, get angry, hit your pillow, grieve, wallow, fear, or stagnate in shock—whatever it takes and wherever it leads. Explore the terrain. Pay attention to the felt-sense of your experience. When you feel that you have gone as deep as you can and you've reached an end that includes the falling away of your emotional energy, stop.

You've freed your energy up as much as conditions allow. If the next step, Internalize, fails to yield results, you've got more to express, explore, embody. You can always come back to this step after time has passed and you've digested what you've experienced so far. Also, new material will often percolate to the surface between sessions, and this added material can help round out, enliven, and lead to resolution in your subsequent work.

CHAPTER SIX

Step 3: Internalize

Remain Still

You've taken your outward expression as far as it could go. Now it's time to internalize it and its accompanying bodily felt-sense. In this step, rather than encouraging sound and movement, you will remain still and hold your experience within. So return now to where you were right before your emotional charge began to dissipate. The idea is to generate as much of that same emotional charge as possible, in stillness, while continuing to pay attention to your body and its cues. You may imagine moving and expressing as you did during the previous step, but you should remain as physically still as possible.

Stay with It

Let's say that in the emotional culmination of the previous step, you experienced fear, accompanied by a sensation of darkness and the bottom falling out. So you now close your eyes and amplify that fear and felt-sense. Allow the sensation of darkness and lack of support to expand. Let it become as expansive as it can get, as fearful, dark, and unsupported as possible. Pump it up. There are no halfway measures here. Do this and follow this method for as long as you can, all the while remaining motionless.

You may begin moving into new emotions or sensations. If this happens, continue to follow and generate them. You may also find that you need to return to outward expression, especially if you are now shifting into unfamiliar territory. In this case, follow the expression process to its end and then move back to internalizing. It's important to heed your intuition and bodily sensations; they will be the most reliable indicators of whether your inner process is on the right track.

Until the End

When you've reached the end of your internalizing process, you'll know it. Your generated emotion and sensations will fade away, and you simply won't be able to produce any more momentum. In effect, you have allowed and embodied all of your emotional message; it is now internalized in your cells, and it is time to move on. You have cleared the deck for what comes next. It's important to remain still while you proceed to the Transform step.

CHAPTER SEVEN

Step 4: Transform

In this step you will again remain still and silent, but now you will pay close attention to the arrival of something new: the transformative state that will solve your problem. But prior to this reshaping of your consciousness, a state of emptiness or nothingness will appear. Ideally during this state of nothingness, the only thought registering in your mind will be that of the nothingness itself, but learning to tolerate unfamiliar states such as emptiness is not always easy. This is because your ego insists on keeping the upper hand by reinforcing the familiar, binding you to preconceived thoughts and habits, and it can mount a variety of responses to keep your mind otherwise engaged.

Usually the first response to emptiness is confusion. How could it not be? A radical shift in consciousness is taking place, and it is shaking your reality. But the very presence of confusion indicates that you are moving into new territory—territory in which you will soon find the illuminating change you seek. So rather than allowing your ego to react and to pull you out of the confusion and into familiar thought patterns, you must learn to tolerate confusion in order to receive what lies beyond. The trick is not to fight the confusion, but to simply let it take place as just another part of your perception and being. Fear of the unknown can also accompany confusion, so you may need to work through this fear before you can reside in unadulterated nothingness. If you're new to listening to your fear and letting it inform you, go back to the Express step for as long as necessary and process your fear. When you have worked with it to its fullest extent and know its terrain, then when you again arrive at the Transform stage, your fear should be much less of a concern. Confusion and fear in the face of nothingness are easily tolerated with practice, especially as you begin to see that nothingness is none other than the harbinger of good things on the immediate horizon.

Your ego's experience of nothingness may bring up further emotions, thoughts, and issues that prevent you from fully accepting it, so you may need to go back to the appropriate step and take up your investigation from there. This is not a race. Jumping past an emotion is counterproductive and leads to convoluted conditions that will be difficult to counter. Always follow and integrate whatever unfolds, in its natural order, even if you have to revisit steps and you feel that you're moving backward. Keep at it. Whatever shows up is there to inform, and paying attention to and resolving seemingly conflicting presences in your consciousness will help you learn to accept emptiness in an attentive but relaxed manner.

When you are able to accept this vacant space, the missing feature of your being will appear and completely resolve your self-development problem. This, the most genuine and precious of gifts, is a true aspect of your soul's greater nature. Its arrival can be overwhelming, all drums and trumpets, but more often it emerges as the "still small voice" of scripture.

Keen and open attention is needed when your higher nature first appears as this subtle presence. Plus, its arrival can be so new and unexpected that you may not recognize it for what it is. A timid emergence may first show itself as a mild physical sensation, a fleeting feeling, a sense of opening, or a vague and distant whisper.

Images, colors, shapes, textures, or smells may present themselves. Because this gentle presence is coming forth after having been shunned for so long, your attention must not push or pull it at all; greet it with only the lightest of touches. If met and followed with kind, patient attention, the sensations will grow and eventually bloom, presenting the full bounty of your truth and the grand and perfect antidote to the problem that has plagued you.

One of a thousand faces of your true, essential nature will present itself, custom-made to compensate for your felt deficiency. You will be entering a new state of being. If you've worked through the fear that had impeded your practice, you may now experience power. If you've harbored hatred toward yourself or another, love or compassion may now dominate your consciousness. But whatever comes up, it will match your needs perfectly. And this quality is not something you will have to coerce into compliance. If peace emerges, you *are* that peace. If compassion emerges, it will take no effort whatsoever to be compassionate, for you *are* compassion. Not only will you experience a compensating state of being, but you might also receive a flood of new insights into your problem, for your emotional self has unlocked the true genius and inspiration of your unfettered mind. This new state of being and accompanying understandings must be experienced to be appreciated or even believed. It is the birth of a new and vibrant self, often centered in the heart—created there through the balanced union of emotions and mind.

Eventually your newfound state will begin to diminish, partly because it's solved your present problem and therefore lost its priority in your awareness, and partly because a lot more work is required before your mind's ego and your sense of identity will allow such fresh takes on reality to become your norm. So in the meantime, there will be more roadblocks requiring further exploration and resolution, but they will present themselves only so that you can go further into the endless realms of actualized self. The more you work this process, the more your identity will shift from your ego to your higher self—and the more you can enjoy the ease of being who you truly are.

CHAPTER EIGHT

Step 5: Unify Through Time

Despite my years of trial-and-error exploration into resolving self-development problems, the definitive and final settlement of many issues remained a conundrum; sometimes I experienced lasting change, and just as often an issue would reappear, no matter what I tried. It seemed as if complete resolution of an issue happened by accident. And these mixed results continued, notwithstanding the application of the Emotion Solution. Although the first four Emotion Solution steps afforded incredible gains in my self-development, gains that opened to realms of spiritual transcendence that would make many a master envious, clearly I was missing something.

Eventually I found it.

To the Rescue

Thanks to the discoveries of neuroscience and the Coherence Therapy research of Bruce Ecker, Laurel Hulley, et al., what has baffled the psychological sciences—the reoccurrence of apparently resolved issues or the lack of an understanding of how to achieve permanent resolution in the first place—is now a thing of the past. While various therapies and techniques could claim cases that reached lasting resolution, they could not claim consistent resolution. But Ecker and company teased out how permanent change is achieved and made that process explicit. Their findings show that when a client uncovers the origins of an issue, and then holds the felt-sense of that original experience in the present while *simultaneously* holding the felt-sense of an experience that contradicts the original experience, the neural track that runs from the present trigger to the historical response dissolves. Although it's meant for psychotherapy, we can adapt this knowledge in the Emotion Solution process to ensure a permanent resolution to the problem impeding our growth. (To learn more about Coherence Therapy and practice, visit CoherenceTherapy.org.)

Adapting these findings to the Emotion Solution is simple, and it is best explained by example. But first you need to understand that this step is conditional; it applies only if your exploration has uncovered the historical origins of your now-resolved problem. Additionally you need to have seen that your original response to the problem was a wise and self-protective act, that it was the best way to maintain your integrity in a threatening environment. If you did explore those roots, you need to complete this step to ensure the permanent resolution of the issue. We will look at a hypothetical case.

Let's say that you could not concentrate and relax during your meditation sessions; in fact, you became anxious. In identifying and processing your anxiety, your exploration took you back to the unsafe, unpredictable environment you suffered while growing up: whenever you tried to relax, your parent behaved aggressively toward you. In response, you became hypervigilant whenever you felt inclined to relax and be at peace. This was the wise, self-protective tactic that you devised, in your youth, to deal with the problem. And although your environment may have changed, to this day the emotional response to your early experience is retriggered whenever you try to relax and concentrate—your meditation sessions being a prime example. So anxious hypervigilance is your present-day symptom.

In the previous Emotion Solution steps, you identified and listened to your anxious self and expressed it; revisited and reexperienced your formative years through mind, emotion, and body; worked with the insanity of growing up in such an environment and the fear and anger involved; observed the wisdom in becoming alert and vigilant in order to protect yourself in your early environment; and saw how this triggers you and affects your present behavior during your meditation practice. And then in transformation, you experienced a deep state of peace and support, a state requiring no vigilance whatsoever, for you are now imbued with the exact conditions required to make relaxation and concentration effortless. Your practice problem is solved. But not quite.

Until now, whenever you tried to relax during practice, you were triggered into your childhood-time-of-danger and your protective response: hypervigilance. Despite the work you just accomplished, this trigger/response track still exists in your brain. So once your newly acquired transformative state of peace and safety eventually loses its predominance and you again need to relax for your practice sessions, this brain circuit can still trigger your on-guard state. In other words, you'll try to relax and concentrate during your meditation session and find yourself back at square one. But the good news is that it is easy to erase this neural track.

Returning to the example, you traced your anxiety back to its origin and experienced the felt-sense of being in danger. In the process you discovered that being hypervigilant as a child was a clever maneuver on your part to protect yourself.

That sums up the past. And now, through your transformation work, you are bathed in a state of peace and support. In the Emotion Solution process, this felt-sense of peace and support will serve as the contrasting experience to the unsafe and unpredictable felt-sense of your childhood.

So these are the two scenarios that you will hold in your awareness simultaneously: being scared and vigilant *and* being supported and peaceful. This is difficult to do perfectly, as your perception will tend to flip from one felt-sense to the other. But do the best you can, for a minute or two. One trick is to imagine your peaceful present self physically holding your scared childhood self, keeping your attention on both felt-senses. Enact this simultaneous holding a few times within the first hour of the Transform stage, and once or twice again within the next several hours.

That's it. The track will disappear. You may have other tracks that lead to that unsafe-environment scenario, but the particular track that distracts you when you try to relax and concentrate during your meditation practice will be gone, for you'll have removed that trigger-response track and unified your present transformation with your past experience. When used within his therapeutic parameters, Ecker calls this process "reconsolidation."

Those are the steps. When you have completed a run-through, enter into your practice routine or just be with yourself in the moment. Notice a difference? It should be striking. Enjoy your progress. And the next time something comes between you and your goals, take a little time to listen, explore, solve the problem, solidify that solution, and finish up by recognizing much more of yourself in the process.

CHAPTER NINE

*Additional Tips and Perspectives
on Opening Emotions*

The following techniques and ideas will increase your ability to put the Emotion Solution into action as successfully as possible.

Emotional backlog operates everywhere in our lives, not only in our self-development practices, but in our everyday interactions and responses to events. We habitually deny or gloss over the emotional forces within our psyches, and in due course we lose depth and capacity to function. Countering the reflexes that diminish our emotional vocabulary and thereby our vitality takes a deliberate act. The following tips, techniques, and perspectives can help you use the capacities of your consciousness to uncover and open to the emotions that facilitate your evolution. While self-development practices are particularly salient means of applying these aids, you can also use them for any life occurrence that prompts an emotional reaction. All you need to do is consciously focus on what is happening to you as an individual within your community and what is taking place on a planetary scale, and then watch for your honest reaction (including the reaction of nonreaction) to uncover emotions you can work with to reclaim your discarded energy. This simple practice of emotional mindfulness can generate a wealth of material through which you can evolve.

Superego Attacks

One method for opening space for a larger, more inclusive sense of self is covered extensively in Byron Brown's book *Soul Without Shame*. This work discusses defending against superego attacks. In short, the superego—sometimes called "the judge" or "the critic"—is the voice in our head saying that we have done something wrong or something right. Our superego tells us that we and others should be one way or another. In particular, it focuses on when, whether, and to what degree certain emotions are acceptable. Far down the road, we seekers will find that we are none other than who we are, and in this purified state of simply being ourselves, there is far less space for self-judgment from the superego. But before then, there is plenty of room for our critic, acting as judge and executioner, to inhibit our ability to simply evolve as ourselves.

Our superego originates as the voice of our parents, caregivers, teachers, religious leaders, institutions, and society in general. These external voices stream a barrage of regulation aimed at fashioning our development in a particular direction. As we mature, however, these voices become "introjects," voices of the critics that formerly have attempted to control us and have now become inner voices that we think are our own. We have absorbed the once-external attacks and directives and made them the foundation upon which we internally regulate and limit ourselves in our present-day lives. Thus, most of us live under constant pressure from our introjected critic;

we must either comply with its demands or react against them. Either way, our critic leaves us little chance to be at rest, for incessant self-monitoring crowds out the freedom of simply being who we are, experiencing life without restraint.

To significantly uncover and grow your truth, you must learn to defend yourself from your critic, and this requires that you first recognize your critic's voice. Sometimes the message will be loud and clear, sometimes barely audible, and sometimes silent and unspoken. In any event, whenever you feel or think that you should be one way or another, that you aren't enough or are too much, or whenever you feel any pressure at all, you can count on the fact that your judge is sending a directive. Recognizing that your critic is holding you in bondage and not letting you be yourself is the first step toward freedom from it. The next step is to assert your authority over it, to defend yourself at any cost.

Your superego is cunning and relentless, and it shows no mercy, so countering this seemingly ever present influence requires cutting it off at the knees. If you try to debate or reason with your superego, it will always win. But there are many ways to effectively defend yourself. One particularly helpful method for defending against an attack, especially in the early stages of learning this self-defense, involves the constructive use of anger.

You should be angry over the imprisonment of your true self, for after all, this voice has successfully severed you from your birthright, your right to be exactly who you are, no strings attached. And the more you realize how much your superego has been controlling and inhibiting your innate being, the more you can employ your indignation to set things right. This is the perfect place to exert your anger, as its righteous use provides the strength you need to keep the critic at bay and win yourself some freedom.

Using anger to defend against your critic is most effective when voiced aloud. If you do not have ready access to that emotion, feign anger toward your critic until your authentic anger kicks in. Or it may be necessary to enlist the aid of a therapist who has worked through their own anger and can thus accept yours; together you can explore why it has become so difficult for you to conjure up anger.

In voicing your anger, simply shut your critic down. An abrupt, volcanic counterattack is often most effective. Sentences that will defend you against your critic (spoken aloud, out of others' earshot) may be something like: "I am sick and tired of listening to your stupid &$#@, day in and day out! Now shut the #%@* up!" Whatever wording seems most appropriate, repeat it for as long as feels fitting. Again, you can fake anger until real outrage kicks in. The idea is to really get your steam up in order to build to a powerful and effective casting out of a foreign presence. Your critic will likely have something to say when you become aggressive, but don't listen to it. Shut it up!

Remember, do not engage the critic in conversation or try to reason with it; it's devious and cannot be trusted. Besides, you are here not to strike a deal, but to get this nag off your back. Some people find it helpful to pretend a pillow is the critic and hit it. Do whatever it takes. This is your true nature, your inherent being at stake. No one or no social order has the right to tell you—or could possibly know, for that matter—who or what you are, or what is true for you.

A defense against your superego can be short and succinct, or it may trigger you into lengthy material—for instance, as when the critic's voice turns into that of one of its originators (e.g., one of your childhood caregivers) and your suppressed anger over their dominating influence becomes available for airing. This is fine. If the session becomes intense, you can merge into the Emotion Solution process and bring your triggered issue to its resolution. This will further break you free of that particular aspect of your critic. In either case—whether you are using your anger to protect yourself from an immediate attack, or you are resolving the original issue—the intent here is to break free of the message. No matter who or what created any particular aspect of your critic's voice, you are now the one taking responsibility for removing your internal conflict and self-censorship.

Most of the time your critic's voice has free rein, cramming your experience with messages and orders telling you who and what you can or cannot be. Its dominance shuts down your sense of openness and possibility. But when you successfully defend yourself, you experience a sense of limitless, clear space that fosters the possibility for change. Taking the time to explore this critic-free sense of freedom is necessary to begin shifting your identity, from one of restraint and inhibition to one of expanse and liberation. Every time you effectively defend yourself against your critic and take the time to experience yourself with its pressure gone, you reinforce your sense of residing in an ambiance of freedom and light, which is a spiritual experience in itself. This sense of gentle expansion also gives you space to stay present with whatever emotion arises. Your openness will last as long as your superego remains in the background. But your inner judge will rush back in to resume its duties the moment you let it, for it is a formidable adversary and will not take kindly to you living without its "guidance." It will return again and again, often with new and elusive twists and turns that make recognizing it and further defending yourself from it an ever evolving task. Your soul needs many new imprints to extricate itself from the worn ruts created by your critic.

There are many other methods for gaining distance from your critic. Interestingly, one method is to tune into and focus your attention on your body. When you do, you ground yourself within your physicality, and your superego (being very much attached to your head) finds itself at a loss. I once counseled a young man who was plagued—tortured, really—by his critic. He could find no relief whatsoever. Knowing that one's superego can gain little foothold when one's attention is consciously embodied, I directed my client to pay close attention to his arms and legs to find the relief he sought. He gave it a try. Suddenly his critic was gone. But he was so accustomed to the ubiquitous voice in his head that before very long at all, he had to terminate the experiment and return to his usual self-criticizing state! Such can be the power of our engrained influences. This client would need to do considerable work before he could tolerate the relief he sought.

Successfully defending against your critic is one of the fastest means for opening the space needed for new experiences. Learning to defend yourself from superego attacks can be a study in itself, and the examples provided here offer but a taste. For those interested in further research and ideas for this practice, Byron Brown's *Soul Without Shame* offers extensive guidance.

Spiritual Superego

What is true for your superego is no less true for your spiritual superego. We all have a little (or maybe not so little) voice that tells us when we are being reverent, when we are not, or in what ways we should be more so. This voice does not seem to diminish after we gain spiritual ground; in fact, it often increases, filled with newfound pride in our success. Again, you need to gain distance from this voice so that you can move forward in your journey. Rather than letting your spiritual superego bask in its own rays and bind you to a stagnant self-image, defend yourself and move on.

Guilt

Guilt can be seen as another type of judge. Much like our superego, it tells us that we cannot be who or what we are, but with a special force: guilt acts as a powerful damper on your emotional energy. Guilt produces nothing. When you listen to your guilt, you will find it to be little more than a suppressing force, squashing the vibrancy of your soul. You can defend yourself by choosing to pay attention to the effect of your guilt and watch it run its course, so you can understand how it operates. Once you have done that, you can dismantle its stunting influence. Simply recognizing that you desire emotional movement and understanding that guilt puts your natural dynamism in a chokehold will help free you from its grip. To be human is to take part in the adventure of self-discovery. Guilt kills the adventure and the discovery. Guilt withholds the energetic quality of being human.

Curiosity

Curiosity provides the drive to search for truth. But few people connect with the whole of their essential curiosity, and so they suffer from limited interest in their experience and evolution. So what is to be done? Trying to cultivate curiosity as a virtue by enlisting your ego to somehow dredge it up will do little good; your ego can produce only an impression of your true and essential curiosity—and a poor impression at that. And because the ego will do anything to preserve itself, it will only glaze over the issues that hold back your inborn curiosity. Since stimulating curiosity head-on through your ego doesn't really work, one recourse is to defuse the energy blocking your inborn curiosity, so it can emerge free from restrictions.

If you were curious as a child, for instance, and your caretakers did not take the time to listen to you, were impatient with your questions, or became angry and ignored you when you asked questions, and you killed your curiosity to please them, then your work is to move through the beliefs, compensations, and emotionally charged structures you created in order to protect yourself from their attacks and lack of support. Dismantling these structures through the Emotion Solution process will allow your curiosity to come out of hiding. Now what previously triggered a stunting of your curiosity will inspire a natural feast of interest.

Start by directly exploring your relationship with your curiosity. Employ the gestalt chair technique. Tell your curiosity what you really think. Beg it to come out, and see how it responds. Or tell it to stay put for its own good. In observing a naturally curious child, what comes up? Again, do whatever it takes and go wherever you feel you are being led. The deeper you go, the more you will liberate your essential curiosity.

Gestalt

A particularly helpful method for including the feeling body in growth work is gestalt therapy. Gestalt strives to engage the client experientially with what is happening in the present moment or with what has occurred in the past as if it were in the present moment. The gestalt therapist works to guide clients to resolution of a presenting issue but, in doing so, knows that there is always a point at which clients become stuck or habitually shy away, leaving their day-to-day issues unresolved. The therapist's job is to keep clients in this part of their process so they can eventually tolerate it and move on to the resolution of their issue. In applying the Emotion Solution to gestalt, this resolution occurs as transformation. You can learn to move through an issue on your own, or, if you prefer, you can work with a therapist who employs an experiential approach such as gestalt. Either way, the major key in processing an issue to its resolution is discovering and dealing with what's "on top."

What's on top is any combination of emotion, thought, or bodily sensation that's actually happening in the moment, as opposed to what we think is happening. Nine times out of ten (to be gracious), the origins and factors at play in an issue are not what we imagine. Identifying what's on top takes considerable practice because we're so used to skirting around and glossing over the emotions, thoughts, and sensations we choose to avoid. Furthermore, what's on top can be the most difficult part of our experience to detect because it can become the very foundation of our experience, something woven into the fibers of our structure and therefore difficult to single out. This inability to see what's on top can become so extreme that we may not have a clue about something others see as our most obvious feature. Working with what's on top is not the new age technique of selecting something positive to hold in your mind and concentrating, but a progressively refined method of being in the moment, without judgment, with whatever is taking place in your experience.

Let's take the well-known example of the interplay between fear and anger. Anger makes some people feel powerful and in control, and so for them, anger is relatively easy to experience. But few people experience anger without some degree of reservation. Imagine a person who, despite the fact that she presents as angry for all the world to see, harbors an unrecognized fear of her anger. Unaware of this dynamic, she habitually defers to the power she gets from acting out her anger, rather than experiencing the lack of power and helplessness associated with her attendant fear. This unaddressed fear may well be sitting on top of her anger, and if it is, she will never fully move through her anger because her access to it will continually be blocked by her unaddressed fear. Consequently, she will experience endless rounds of persistent fear-impregnated anger. If she was able to fully accept and experience her anger, it would change into something else, such as power or strength—an essential quality that she has been missing and for which her anger has been trying to compensate. But with fear on top of her anger, she can never move beyond partial success at processing that anger.

When you try to move past what's on top, you're wasting your time. Worse, by avoiding an emotion like the fear that is on top, you'll actually draw more fear-producing situations into your life, situations that you will probably react to with even more anger. Only after you accept and move through your on-top fear can you accept and move through your underlying anger.

The above example may be the opposite for some people; they can habitually experience fear when anger is what's really on top. And of course there can be, and often are, many more layers and permutations involved in getting down to the heart of a matter. In any case, paying attention to the nuance that we normally gloss over will eventually lead to the truth of the issue, making resolution possible.

Discerning what's on top in any particular instance is probably easiest to accomplish by noticing physical cues. The axiom "The body does not lie" earns its badge here. Your mind may attempt to figure things out, but it can produce and get stuck in all manner of concoction and projection. Your body cuts straight to the truth.

A thinly veiled gesture can reveal the anger behind depression, anxiety behind a self-assured facade, grief leaking through a sunny disposition. While it is often easier for another person to detect your self-deceptions, the more you learn to pay attention to your body's nuances, the more you can pick up on its cues.

Your mind has a lot to say and will happily give all manner of explanation in your explorations, but there are times to ignore your mind and let your often-neglected body and emotions take the reins and guide you to your truth. This isn't to say your mind has nothing to offer; in its proper place, it does. Eventually your mind will find that place and give equal space to your heart, emotions, and body; but until then suspect the domination exerted by your mind—the part of you that might not cooperate in discovering which of your experiences is on top.

Everything Is Projection

An effective method for clarifying inner structures is adopting the idea that "everything is projection." The concept is simple: everything we see outside of ourselves, along with how we experience it, originates from within. Or put another way: what we see in others and the world and how we judge and interpret what we see are exactly how we see, judge, and interpret ourselves. Or from yet another angle: we take what we can't accept about ourselves and project it out onto other people and the world at large, where we treat it as a problem foreign to our constitution. We also take what we like about ourselves and project it out onto others—but because it's favorable, we identify with it. Either way, the outcome is the same: we can barely see reality as it exists beyond our own projections.

At first, this perspective may seem outlandish, but the more you work with it, the more you'll find its value. If you can at least entertain the possibility that whatever you see, think, feel, or suspect to be another's motives is actually what motivates you, you will have tremendous fodder to work with. By understanding that what we critique in our outer world are the conditions or issues we hold within ourselves, we can accept the fact that we are entirely responsible for what we create and how we view the world. It also demonstrates how we keep ourselves separate from the All of Creation, for whatever we view as other than ourselves is precisely what prevents us from experiencing the inclusiveness of the All. The more we work through our issues and move closer to recognizing the truth of what actually is, devoid of projections, the less "everything is projection" seems like a horribly narcissistic orientation, and the more it becomes a valid guide.

For example, you might judge an acquaintance as helpless and write him off. He can't seem to take care of himself, he forever appears to be a victim, and he can't seem to do anything about it. You find this helplessness unacceptable, something with which you could never identify. But if you assume that his helplessness is a reflection of the helplessness you can't accept within yourself, you open up a world of possibility.

In this case, your buried assessments of your own helplessness are laid bare before you. If you have the courage to face this bellwether of self-hatred and then do the work to move through your repulsion toward your own helplessness, you'll not only find self-acceptance, but you'll also find that your acquaintance's helplessness is no longer a concern of yours at all. You are no longer projecting your self-hatred onto this person, and you can relate to him in a straightforward, reality-based manner, just as you can now better relate to yourself. Helplessness is now just one of your acquaintance's characteristics, part of his humanity, as it is part of your own—something everybody possesses to one degree or another. The further you take "everything is projection," the more you'll see and merge with other people and the world as they actually are.

Turn It Around

People who work at emotional integration often find that much of "common knowledge" is backward: if we turn much of what we believe, see, and hear around 180 degrees, we come closer to the truth.

Consider this turn-it-around method in relation to the concept of positive affirmations, which remain popular despite the argument and evidence that affirmations don't really work. This is no big surprise when viewed through the lens of how many denials there are and how denied energy perpetuates. But by turning it around, you can use positive affirmations to your advantage and make them many times more serviceable to your growth.

Look at the work of Louise Hay. In her popular book *Heal Your Body*, she lists different types of ailments and malaise, along with the emotional and belief systems that lie behind them. She then offers affirmations meant to counter those beliefs and emotions—affirmations that purportedly lead to healing. While this may seem to work for those with a particularly strong mental constitution (notwithstanding the ailment rearing its head through a different symptom), the relief is usually temporary and leaves us none the wiser. Thorwald Dethlefsen and Ruediger Dahlke, in their book *The Healing Power of Illness: Understanding What Your Symptoms Are Telling You*, profess that the symptoms of an illness hold important messages that, when identified and acted upon, lead not only to physical health, but also to psychological and spiritual development. They advocate seeing the symptoms of illness for what they are and exploring them from that viewpoint, rather than working against them, as is advised in Hay's work.

Hay's affirmations, however, can be extremely accurate and helpful (and more in line with Dethlefsen and Dahlke's view) when turned around 180 degrees. There are two ways to reverse Hay's suggestions and make them effective. The first is to say aloud the affirmation as it stands, and then, rather than forcing yourself to feel and think what the affirmation suggests, let yourself feel and think what you actually feel and think in *reaction* to the unreality posed by the affirmation—the polar opposite of what Hay suggests. If you feel weak and the affirmation tells you to profess your strength, you can use this dichotomy to contrast and accentuate the weakness that you *actually* feel. Your gut reaction to Hay's positive affirmation helps define an accurate and straightforward picture of the true beliefs and emotions in play. Now, with your honest response, you have material to investigate, process, and fully integrate. The 180-degree affirmation has helped you move closer to the message underlying your illness.

The second way you can use Hay's work is by affirming the opposite of what she suggests. Rather than saying something to counter your present state, such as "My body is healed, and I am filled with positive light that is reflected throughout my being," you can say, "My body is degenerating, and I am filled with negativity that is reflected throughout my being." Ha! While this approach may sound strange, the first step in dealing effectively with any problem is to admit you have it. Once you admit your condition, the thought forms and emotional energy that need to be integrated present themselves. The journey proceeds from this point. Attempting to fool your mind into believing something it doesn't believe or into feeling something you don't feel will just force your emotional energy to find further means of expression, in ever more desperate attempts to reveal the truth behind your problem. Another example of this counterproductive approach is meditating with the intention of persuading yourself that you are calm and centered to negate your anxiety. Instead, go with the flow; meditate on the fact that you are agitated and scared. Follow those emotions to find the calm and centeredness that you seek. This process is fast, effective, and lasting, much more so than it would be if you were using manipulative means to contradict your symptom.

If you do anything to divert yourself from where you honestly are in the moment, you're trying to bypass your true self. If you want to experience more peace, the answer is not to take up your ego's idea of peace and somehow become peaceful, for you are then trying to be something you are not. Your mind cannot really conjure up a state such as peacefulness; it's terrible at it. Rather, this is an opportunity to use your mind, in conjunction with your emotions and body, to investigate. What is holding peace at bay? Do you feel grief because you're other than peaceful? If so, go into that grief, and process and transform it. Why do you even think you should be peaceful? Is it the "spiritual" way to be? If you are agitated at this moment, what's wrong with that? What are the judgments and feelings around your agitation? What is it really like to fully experience agitation in your body? What occurs when you accept your agitation and just let it be? The paradox is that if you allow yourself to experience how much you want peace and how much you don't have it, rather than pretending that you possess it, you can move much closer to the true peace you seek: natural and essential peace, rather than a forced quasi-peace instilled by your ego.

The method of "turning it around" can also be used in practices such as acceptance. Instead of trying to change your mind into accepting what you cannot accept, a common practice that leads to partial success at best, why not work with the fact that you can't accept it? Once you embrace your nonacceptance, you can move through the thoughts and the emotions that hold your resistance in place and let true acceptance come on its own. The same can be said for forgiveness. True forgiveness comes when the emotional charge you feel when you hold something against someone is integrated and transformed within your being; then you actually *are* forgiving, rather than someone who *performs* a forgiving act. Mentally forcing your heart to open to forgiveness runs a paltry second to the essential forgiveness gained through doing the 180-degree opposite of what most forgiveness experts promote.

Victim/Perpetrator

If it's true that we are all composed of both shadow and light, then it stands to reason that we have both perpetrator and victim within us. But while this may be so, most people tend to favor one over the other: some habitually play the victim, while others favor the role of the perpetrator. If you find yourself favoring one of these positions when you're exploring issues and their emotional content, and you're not experiencing much progress reaching the goal of changing, try inhabiting the victim/perpetrator position that you normally avoid. This approach will bring your process to life.

If you are usually the victim, take the perpetrator stance. Get into the emotions around it. As this may be new ground for you, start by acting as if you were the perpetrator in the present moment. You are now the culprit, the source of what has been done to you or your world. Work it up and don't give up; authentic perpetrator attitudes and emotions will eventually take over (they're in there, waiting to be heard).

If you rarely take the victim stance, usually preferring to identify with the power of the aggressor by mistreating another person, take on the part of victim, as if you were the one subjected to the abuse you normally dish out. Get into it. Point your finger in outrage, timidly cower, or fall into helplessness at what has been done to you. This role is a part of you as much as anything else, so you might as well start owning and inhabiting it to see where it leads.

When you thoroughly investigate and accept the less favored side in a particular issue, especially if you use the Emotion Solution, both sides begin to lose their distinct qualities. They become nondual; once you stop identifying with either side of the coin, the two sides become nothing but the coin itself. This is not to say that you won't be able to distinguish the victim from the perpetrator in daily life; rather, you'll better understand both sides and see how they fit together to make a whole. You'll also become less prone to acting out either side. Now you're much closer to experiencing a dynamic as it actually exists, rather than through the limits of your judgments and habitual preferences. And you'll be that much closer to experiencing yourself through the inclusiveness of your true nature.

Merge Polarities

Merging polarities is a technique that can be useful when you're vacillating or stuck between two sides of an issue. An example might be when you alternately love and hate someone, with not much in between, despite opening up to and processing those conflicting emotions. Or you may find yourself of two minds, feeling joyful about living on Earth and falling into despair over the prospects of life here. Our truth probably lies somewhere between these two poles: we love some things about someone and are really ticked off by other things; life on Earth can be both joyful and full of despair. Or stated differently, when we are able to experience and grasp the truth of this instance, what was previously an either-or dichotomy now comes closer to being a united whole. A shortcut that sometimes proves effective for experiencing this higher truth of integration involves inwardly holding any two polarities of an issue together, at the same time.

Keeping polarities in your attention at the same time will work only if you have fully explored, as in the first case, both your love and your hatred of the person in question, only when you have gained the ability to feel, hold, and express these two emotional states outwardly and separately, each in its own right. Then you can merge the two poles. The method itself is straightforward: sit silently and hold the opposing positions and emotions, thoughts, and felt-sense in your consciousness at the same time, without judgment, while paying close attention to your body and what may develop there. This takes a little practice, similar to that required by the Unify step of the Emotion Solution. Just do the best you can. If some form of synthesis appears, stay with this new awareness, making sure to remain grounded in your body. Let it lead where it will, if it wants to lead you anywhere at all. You may be surprised at the changes in perception this simple technique provides.

Resistance

You can also look at your personal development in terms of resistance: if you're not in contact with the totality of your nature, you're experiencing some form of resistance to it. Becoming enlightened, self-realized, whole, or aware of your true, unbounded nature is little more than becoming consciously aware of what you have always been. So becoming cognizant of your true nature is gaining the ability to experience who and what you actually are, without resistance.

Resistance to the truth of who and what you are is multilayered and deep, but always tied to your emotional body. While erring thoughts play an important role in keeping us separated from the truth of our being, emotions are the energy that keeps these thoughts intact. Working directly with the energy behind our resistance gives us unparalleled ability to come into contact with our truth. Working with resistance is just another form of going with what is, in the present moment. When you sense your resistance toward something in your experience, work with the beliefs and emotions around that resistance. You are dealing, once again, with actuality. After you've let your resistance say everything it has to say by letting your emotions run their course, the mental structures around the particular form of resistance will fall apart.

For example, imagine that you are trying to lose weight but feel you don't have the courage to carry you to your goal. Look at this example from the perspective that you have everything you need, including the fortitude to achieve a goal such as losing weight; it is part of your innate being. Then it stands to reason that if you are experiencing anything short of that mettle, you are exhibiting some sort of resistance to it. So what is your resistance to your inner strength? Explore the space between you and it. Does that strength seem distant? Does your resistance have substance and texture, or is it an introjected voice calling you weak? Or do you simply have a sense that fortitude is unattainable? If that's the case, allow yourself to explore that sense of unattainability. It may seem vague or illusory at first, but go for the emotion behind it. Or do you feel helpless to lose weight? If so, inhabit that helplessness and follow wherever it leads you. Your relationship with your missing quality, such as strength, always includes a form of resistance to it. Follow that energetic charge, and embody it so that you can dismantle the mental belief or program that keeps you from being able to draw from your essential fortitude. Conscious and unconscious resistances will always appear when you attempt to improve yourself. Get to know and truly inhabit these resistances, and your progress will unfold on its own.

Avoidance

If you are serious about living in contact with your emotional self, eventually you must face how many of your activities and habits are designed to hold you back from that very contact. Some of these may include obvious means to hide from your feelings: overeating, excessive entertainment, compulsive social activities, drugs, and so forth. Other forms of escape may not be so obvious—the constant static of your mind, or your habit of retreating into the folds of a preferred emotional state to escape what you don't want to face. For fear of possible failure, you might use tactics such as replacing your desire with resignation so that you can hide from feelings associated with hope. The permutations are manifold. The further you travel, the more you'll see how much of your life is fashioned to avoid certain emotional states.

If you are aware of an avoidance pattern, you can choose to stop the avoidance and then tune in to what happens. Maybe you get the urge to eat when you're not hungry as a means of avoidance. Don't succumb to that urge; rather, accept the emotions and sensations that come up in food's absence. Or maybe you avoid your unwanted emotions with excessive busyness. Instead of racing through the entire day at breakneck speed, take some time to stop and sit with what comes up in reaction to slowing down; emotions are bound to show themselves. Or you can go with and exaggerate your avoidant behavior to better understand it. Race around at top speed while paying attention to what you are doing. Another example might be that you project a confident attitude to mask insecurities that lie beneath it. Go with that persona and walk around as confidently as possible. You can even give a passionate speech out loud on the effectiveness of your feigned confidence. Let your avoidance behavior shine, and see where it leads. Whatever your pattern, look at how much time you spend each day evading contact with aspects of yourself and what this says about your relationship with yourself. Increasing your awareness of an avoidance pattern and working with its emotional charge will break it down.

When opening to what underlies your avoidant behavior, treat yourself with respect. Don't overwhelm yourself. Avoidance patterns are there for a reason, and removing them needs to be done progressively, one step at a time. It is all too easy to beat yourself up for not sufficiently facing yourself, and then pull too much of your compensating behavior away at one time, all in the name of becoming more healed or spiritual. When you experience this form of self-hatred, defend yourself with the admonishment that you refuse to hurt yourself in the name of healing, and tell your superego or spiritual superego to get lost. At a later date you can inquire why you pressure yourself to be something other than what you are. Gently allow into your consciousness the emotions beneath your avoidance patterns, working with just enough to digest at a comfortable, safe rate.

Journaling

Journaling is a popular way to keep in contact with and more open to your emotional self. Some people find that journaling during their transformational experience keeps the process more objective; it becomes a form of witness, especially if they're working alone. Others find that writing down what occurs during the actual work takes away from the flow of emotions, and that journaling after their experience works best. Still others find speaking into a recording device beneficial.

Witnessing

A witness, in the form of a trusted friend or therapist, can help actualize and objectify your process. If you choose to work with a friend or professional, they must have worked through the presenting issue themselves. The mere presence of a fellow seeker, if they are able to witness and nonjudgmentally reflect back what they see, can enhance your objectivity and grounding for an enriched perspective on your present state.

Breathing and Other Body-Oriented Techniques

Many body-oriented techniques are designed to open us to our sensate and emotional bodies. In choosing one, it's important to keep in mind that some body-oriented methods can open you too quickly to repressed, suppressed, and unconscious material, or material that cannot currently be assimilated. No good comes from opening too fast, too soon. There are certainly practitioners who might argue otherwise or won't take your safety into consideration. As in all aspects of life, listen to your inner guidance and look out for yourself.

To reiterate: A professional will be able to support you only in the experiences that they themselves have worked through and assimilated into their own psyche. Otherwise they'll push you out of your experience and leave you floundering. This is human nature and cannot be helped. If this happens to you, it's time to move on, find another therapist, or work on your own.

Salient Points to Remember
Throughout Your Explorations

• The mind must blend in perfect balance with the emotions, through the physical body, the condition that creates true heart. Focusing on any one element leads to a contorted outcome. This book is meant to help you focus on the neglected state of your emotions; however, it doesn't advocate favoring your emotional body over your mind, body, or heart. It does suggest using extra effort to bring your emotions back to life, and this may include favoring emotions over the mind for a period of time so that the emotional body can open up and take its rightful place. Ultimately, this work is not about being a slave to any one part of self, but engaging all parts as equals.

• All emotions are natural and necessary for a fulfilling life.

- You cannot hate or fear an emotion and at the same time accept that emotion.

- When you discover that you avoid an emotion, first process the emotion fueling that avoidance.

- Desiring an emotion to change is in direct conflict with accepting that emotion. Wanting it to change, however slightly, may lead to partial success in the short term but failure in the long term. It's better to explore why you want to change the emotion, which is a valid part of you just as it is.

- Desiring one emotion over another is nothing less than internal dictatorship, but paying attention to and working with the desire to experience one emotion over another leads to self-knowledge and opens the way to accepting the resisted emotion.

- Denying an emotion ensures its continued adverse influence. Accepting an emotion ensures your evolution.

- There is no need to be other than what you are. There is no reason to feel other than what you feel. If thoughts or emotional reactions intrude to argue against these two points, investigate until you inhabit the emotional charge around the encroaching element and experience transformation into your essential, true nature—the freedom to be the one and only you.

CHAPTER TEN

Integrating Emotions into Your Current Practice

The Emotion Solution offers insightful ways of evaluating the strengths and weakness of other self-development techniques.

There are many roads to achieving a self-development goal, but few who follow these roads achieve satisfaction. Most give up in frustration or settle for partial success. The major reason behind their failure is that self-help disciplines and their proponents fail to acknowledge the contribution of the emotional body to the same extent that they accept the contribution of the mind, and so their attempts at growth suffer. But the good thing is that you can act on your own behalf and include emotional acceptance into virtually any self-development work. In doing so, you may choose to hide the inclusion from a conventional teacher, but once you've experienced sweeping progress, you won't care.

Welcoming emotions into your work adds a dynamism that can be breathtaking. Your emotions *want* to help you realize more; they propel you forward and become the keys to cascading breakthroughs. Emotions inform and tailor your practice to your individual needs—needs powered by your emotions themselves. And your emotions tell you when a discipline, as a whole, is not working for you and when you need to move on, for, after all, emotions offer the best selective process. But nothing convinces like the doing.

What follows is a list of self-development practices with examples of how to apply the Emotion Solution to their techniques. It is a general list. There are many practices and variations of such, but this will give you an idea which direction to take in emotional adaptation within a system, with fine-tuning left to the reader. I point out weaknesses regarding each practice's relative exclusion of emotions and offer suggestions for incorporating emotional acceptance. But you'll come up with methods to fit your unique self. That is both the challenge and the fun of it.

Creative Arts

When given full rein, creative expression is one of the surest means to plunge into the task of finding your inner truth. Various emotions come up during the creative process, and the more creators grapple with them and grow, the better and the more evocative the fruits of their labor. But creators, like all people, fall prey to the judgment, denial, and suppression of major parts of their emotional selves and thus inhibit their creative expression.

Raising the emotional bar through creative acts speaks for itself. Gaining more humanity through enhanced union with self and world affords the artist a corresponding range of vision and creative expression; there is simply more to express and more vital material from which to draw. But in the meantime, lack of inspiration, frustration, feelings of inability, and other blocks to creativity can get in the way. Pick from the following suggestions to get your emotion-driven juices going.

- Freak out. While many schools will tell you not to freak out over a hindrance to your creative production and suggest palliative practices to guide you through and around blocks, why not try freaking out? Let it go, follow your freak-out to the origin of your block, and then transform it into the very energy whose lack imposed that block.

- Take on frustration. If you feel frustrated with your work, rather than choosing an avoidance technique or one meant to allow you the breathing room to invite something new, take on your frustration. See how it feels in your body. Concentrate on those sensations and let them evolve. Odds are you were frustrated in the past and the tendrils of that frustration are reaching out into your present moment. Follow them back to the felt-sense of their origins. Maybe a caregiver wouldn't allow you to finish projects or gave you the message that you don't have a creative bone in you. Process what comes up as if it were occurring right now, in the moment. Investigate the atmosphere of the frustration. Maybe you feel as if you're surrounded by fog, or you feel pressure coming at you from all sides and can't get away. Amplify those feelings. See if and how they change and what they have to say. Taking frustration just as it is will lead to freedoms virtually unobtainable through other means.

- Set a goal and watch what happens. Perhaps you're a writer and you can't write that proverbial first sentence. State your goal out loud, and then, while attempting to write, tune into your body and emotions. Go from there. Maybe you instantly judge yourself. Explore that impulse. Or maybe a cavernous void opens before you, threatening to swallow you up. Hold the felt-sense of the experience and ride it out. Or maybe you just want to kick and scream. Do it. Go with whatever comes up, as long as you stay safe. Or maybe a voice says that you will never be a writer. Listen to it. Become the person who first issued that paralyzing edict and dressed your (younger) self down, as if the conversation were occurring now, and discover what you're taking on.

- Ask yourself what your life would be like if you were a prolific, successful writer or visual artist. Embody the felt-sense of that image. How do you react? Is it in contrast to your usual felt-sense? This is an exercise that propels you to face your blocks and the history that established them.

Dance and Movement

It's obvious that expressive dance and movement are greatly facilitated and become more fluid when inspired by the emotional body, just as emotional expression is inhibited and wooden when consciousness is overly dominated by fixed ideas and images, and by lack of feeling. In the latter case, you are left with presentations composed of hashed-over, worn-out past experience, a sorry replacement for inspiration derived from something new springing from the soul. And nothing inspires like being in the moment and open to whatever moves through your perception, made available for translation through your body.

Adding inner exploration that includes the free flow of emotions, as laid out in the Emotion Solution process, increases the capacity to find and act through a revitalized, unique self. Nothing lays better groundwork for the spontaneous and the new. By processing your inhibitions, you'll find balance and expression through your heart, a heart that will become spontaneous, adaptive, and vital. Your enhanced range of inner touch will move outward, toward your audience.

In dance and movement, as in other creative arts, confronting your blocks offers the most direct route to spontaneity and originality. Exaggerate those blocks. Let them speak. Argue with them. They are already exhibiting themselves through your body; investigate what they are trying to say. Dance or move in a prescribed way and pay attention to how you feel. Are you curious, intrigued, angry, afraid, unsure? Expressing what restricts you through your body is a particularly effective means of realizing a more expansive self.

Devotional Practices

Devotion is considered here as a general category, composed of the practices that devotees use when they try to emulate and to merge with the object of their devotion, be it God or God's representatives or emissaries. Devotion to nature is also included. In dedication, admiration, and love, many of the world's religious doctrines abide. When enlightenment or grace is considered a reward of devotion, it appears when nothing stands between the devotee and the object of their love.

Obvious problems show up in devotional practices. One is that the worshiper must rely on their ego's image of devotion and love, an image that might not be as trustworthy as they might think. Actually it's not trustworthy at all. True devotional love, like all kinds of love, is conveyed through the heart. If what comes from your heart isn't the natural product of the balance between emotions and intellect, it remains an image generated by your biased, unenlightened ego. This puts the major vehicle of devotional love in question: you're seeking to emulate a preconceived image of divine love whose characteristics and functioning you can't imagine.

But there is a solution. When you do the work to access your essential love, a love that forever remains out of your ego's reach, your devotion becomes an evolving jewel of its own making. Emotional acceptance alone gives rise to pure devotional love because it addresses and clears the structures your ego placed between you and that love. Only this transformation leads to a clean merging with the object of desire.

As the Emotion Solution advises, instead of trying to love devotedly when you can't do so, give air to the elements that impede your devotion. Or try to worship while admitting that you don't know what devotion is or how to attain it. Once again, when you work with these seemingly self-negating inadequacies, more of your authentic, non-ego-driven self becomes available, affording you the capacity to authentically merge with the object of your devotion.

Another shortcoming is that devotional practices tend to dismiss, to one degree or another, thoughts and feelings that are contrary to the doctrine, to the results of the doctrine, or to the beliefs of an administrator or representative of the doctrine. In other words, if you find something suspect, you are encouraged to downplay your response, as questioning is rarely encouraged in devotional practices. Again, this stance cuts you off from the rewards of investigating the fullness of your subjective experience and thus finding an effective, individualized solution to your problem. It does nothing less than encourage self-diminishment, curbing your capacity to foster all-encompassing devotion.

The ideas that God or Mother Nature might withhold her wealth from someone who questions and that it is ungodly or goes against nature to question hold no water. God does not like questions? How can we accept the idea of a god that does not question itself or allow admirers to question it? Aren't we trying to rid the world of the power figures who do just that? Offering your devotion without questioning and without paying attention to your reactions by shoving them under the rug to molder is foolish. Engage your curiosity and ask questions in your devotional practice, no matter how contentious they may seem, and you'll be free to devote yourself with the fullness of your being.

Inquiry: The Path of Self-Examination

This is the path on which the seeker attempts to know self directly, for its own sake. The more you come to understand what makes you tick and work through your issues in the day-to-day world, the more baggage you will remove and the clearer your naked personal truth will become. Because you are part of a greater whole, the more you know your own truth, the more you'll come to know the truth of an inclusive consciousness. This book is especially helpful to seekers who desire to know the whole of who they are. Self-inquiry, with the full inclusion of one's emotional self, best facilitates this process.

Karma Yoga

Karma yoga concerns right living: living with good thoughts, words, and deeds. Possessing these qualities is believed to lead to a virtuous and happy life. All focus is on action; the yogi focuses on work performed, without regard to outcome, and thus is free from the craving for success. And it's said that putting all your attention on the process and not the end result ensures the best chance at happiness in life.

The difficulty here is that in order to have a good life, the yogi has to lose all attachments to gaining that good life. What's never considered is that the fastest way for them to do this is to directly investigate the constellation of structures surrounding their ego's desire for a good outcome, and dismantle (resolve) these structures in the process.

Try feeling how much you crave a good life and how much unhappiness you actually experience. Are you harboring fear, anger, resentment, frustration? Allow the emotion and move through it; do not ignore it or force yourself past it. The yogi who could work through all the steps of the Emotion Solution would come in contact with their essential nature; and from this enlightened perspective, they could naturally function with the least possible influence from ego. When the yogi is operating from this new place, the doing truly becomes the doing regardless of outcome, for the yogi has moved into a state of being. And interestingly, this "doing" state of being is neither dependent upon nor concerned with degrees of happiness. Looking into the ego's issues through the full inclusion of emotions would cut years off the yogi's efforts to live without regard for an outcome.

Living Life as It Is

A close cousin to living an examined life is, paradoxically, living life as it is. Life holds all you need to evolve as a human being. Fully respond to what you have drawn into your personal life and what occurs in the life around you. This is both your prescription and your cure. Simply living your life in ever increasing consciousness may be the bare-bones path to enlightenment, but this approach leaves nothing to be desired. We live and contribute more of ourselves through aware involvement, through progressing and reclaiming more of ourselves in self-discovery. We become less prone to acting out because we've uncovered, taken in, and provided safe harbor for our energy. And as in karma yoga, we become less concerned with an outcome because we are in the moment of involved doing.

Simply living life, aware and moving in balance with all aspects of our nature, calls forth our highest self. We find and inhabit our place in humanity. Though often invisible to others, this is among the finest ways to contribute to the general welfare.

Meditation

Arguably, meditation can be described as taming the mind and emotions through the discipline of mind. Most aspirants see this process as clearing the way to higher and more peaceful states of consciousness. And in many ways it does—but at a certain cost to your emotional self. While meditation may take an emotional toll on those who identify with their intellect, for those who primarily operate through their emotions, the cost is much more exorbitant. After all, meditation focuses mainly on the mind, while it discounts emotions. But nobody needs to sacrifice part of their nature in order to experience meditative states. Quite the opposite is true.

Meditation may be valuable, but even those who have been doing it for years find it less productive than they would like. And interestingly, adherents rarely employ techniques to accelerate their progress. Yet meditation can become easier and far more productive than most people could imagine. Enter the Emotion Solution.

Many meditation techniques train you to let invading thoughts, sensations, and emotions gently float by as you return your focus to something else, such as your breathing or a mantra. Essentially, you are to clear your mind or, at least, lose attachment to whatever thoughts and emotions arise. But for most people (especially the emotionally oriented) this is difficult. After all, our emotions and their energy, as well as thoughts that contain an emotional charge, beckon us. As they should.

Emotions have important information to convey. Always. So why not allow them to contribute their transformative power during meditation? We're taught not to engage our emotions during meditation, but what if our teachers are simply repeating what they were taught? What if the methods they perpetuate contain such a masculine bias that their teaching is much less effective than it could be? This is sacrilege, you say? Even if you think it is, you owe it to yourself to try the following approach and find out.

By all means meditate. But while doing so, pay attention to what your mind is doing and how it affects your meditation. Notice your emotions. And importantly, notice any patterns in how you *react* to those observations. Don't let your own judgments about your activity go by unnoticed.

Say you are meditating and you can't seem to implement what you've been told to do. You've been trained to meditate a certain way, but you're frustrated because you don't get it, you can't seem to get anywhere, or you are stuck—and no matter how much you try (or, as they say, "don't try"), you just can't get there. The suggestion here is to allow, in fact encourage, your emotional response to your lack of success and follow it. This necessitates breaking the rules of most meditation practices, but you can do it undetected while you sit unmoving and silent. Besides, you can always return to your usual meditation routine and suffer no loss.

So if you realize that you're at your wit's end and plagued by frustration, welcome that frustration. Let it build and dominate your awareness. Hold it. Watch it. Try to feel your frustration to the *n*th degree. See where it goes—if indeed it wants to go anywhere. After you have fully entertained and absorbed whatever is occurring, it will subside and change. Pay attention to any changes and accompanying realizations. Pay attention to your body and the overall atmosphere. In others words, employ the Emotion Solution process, but entirely in stillness and silence. Stay with the process until it thoroughly resolves your problem by allowing you to reach transformation and unify. Then go back to your regular meditation. When you do, you may be in for a real eye-opener. Working with your emotional body, rather than trying to downplay it during meditation, can lead to advances in your meditation practice that you (and your teachers) never dreamed possible.

Mindfulness (also see Practicing Presence and Being in the Now)

In discussing mindfulness, we will focus on its core practice and, of course, on its relationship to emotions. Mindfulness: full of mind. Proponents tell us to accept emotions but not to identify with, express, or react to them. This is accomplished through mental discipline. There is no clearer example of one part of selves, our mind, lording it over another part, our emotions.

The traditional process of mindfully "accepting" emotions has four parts: First, we recognize that we have a particular emotion. Second, we name it—both to keep us from identifying with the emotion and to keep the emotion "uncomplicated" by our reactions and therefore easier for the mind to observe. Third, we "unconditionally accept" the emotion by letting it be and simply experiencing it in our body, and by acknowledging that it has arisen due to certain conditions. (This way we don't take the emotion "personally.") Fourth, we mentally investigate the emotion through our bodily sensations of it in the present moment; the body becomes the container of the emotion, disconnected from any other thing that may be associated with the emotion. Through this process, we come to a place where we don't react to our emotions, and thus we can interact with the world objectively, without being overwhelmed by our feeling body.

I find the above scenario disturbing. Imagine a detached, in-his-head, nonresponsive "mindful" husband observing and mentally figuring out his emotional wife, dispassionately sizing her up, categorizing her, and then placing his results on a shelf, so he'll remain forever indifferent toward her. Meanwhile his wife continues to exhibit her disquieting emotional nature, begging to be seen and heard, only to find herself never truly acknowledged. Now you have an accurate picture of how our internal polarities are supposed to relate to each other during traditional mindfulness practice. Not all forms of mindfulness are that biased, but the fact that so many people buy into this view is sad testimony to the prejudices we harbor.

While, no doubt, many who encourage traditional mindfulness practices may have good intentions and produce some favorable results, they also cause harm. The biggest problem comes in identifying reactions to emotions as undesirable. It is through our reactions that we find the depth of our humanity; our reactions direct us and open the door. And mindfulness adherents do not appear to make a clear distinction between acting out emotions and responsibly responding to them and taking them in—as if the two different approaches were the same thing with the same end result. One conclusion is clear: mindfulness guidelines assume that if we actually go with our emotions in our daily practice, nothing good will come of it. Implicit here are the assumptions that our rational self is superior to our emotional self and that it knows what to do with those pesky emotions. Hatred of the feminine polarity is another way to put it. But as those who have learned to include the fullness of their emotions in their mindfulness practice can attest, only when you reach the point of emotional fluidity in your practice can you experience the greatest rewards.

If we simply let our emotions pass by without reacting to and identifying with them, we lose their message and thus a chance to expand our awareness. Reacting to (not acting out) your emotional impulses is following the spearhead of your authentic being. Your reaction to an emotion is just that: your reaction, no less a part of your being than anything else. The triggering event and your emotional reaction to it are highly personal. How can you investigate or come to terms with your nature without knowing the full extent of your reactions? If you are triggered into a reaction and then force yourself to remain neutral to the emotion involved, you are never going to gain the benefit from that trigger. It goes to waste. Not to mention that the emotional energy you are not taking "personally" is still affecting you personally, whether you like it or not. Your reactions will change and subside when you work with your emotions as they arise, much more so than when you just let them pass by, because you are fully responding to what is happening inside you and allowing it its rightful place in your evolution. What mindfulness pioneers say has worked for them may not be in your best interest, especially when they claim to follow a path of love and compassion, for they derive their methods from a position that discounts the emotional half of their nature. They really need to figure out that recognizing emotions and then winking at them from a superior position is not the same as loving and integrating them.

And they won't attain a truly loving and compassionate state until they accept and deal with what they've failed to recognize within themselves: the lack of heart they display toward their emotional, feminine nature, no matter how much they profess love and compassion. True and essential compassion and love naturally flow from first owning and transforming what inhibits their presence, and so often that is the energy of hatred and heartlessness—something we all possess, like it or not. When the true-nature form of love and compassion arrives, it becomes a normative state of being, no more or less important than any other aspect of your nature, and certainly nothing to promote above any other essential state of being; when the promoters of compassion and love come to possess the real thing, they will stop arguing for it.

Mindfulness experts do teach us to recognize emotions as part of us, but usually only a part to remain impersonal toward and keep in compliance with the dictates of the mind. Consider instead taking emotions personally. Respond. React. See where this leads. See what your emotions have to say about you and the world in which you live. Include those emotions associated with your desire to become mindful. So rather than letting emotions pass by, investigate them. Express them. Look into them as valuable and informative. Let them do what they do and go where they go, with the whole of you. Use mental control to *allow* your emotions. Start with more surface emotions, if this process is new to you. Or if at first you have to keep some distance between you and your emotions, so be it. Notice the distance. But eventually you'll find your process needs increasing intimacy with your depths. With the addition of emotions to your mindfulness practice, you can keep the parts of it that help you and drop those that hamper you. See what works.

Mysticism

Many of mysticism's practices use self-discipline and self-convincing to help the adherent become virtuous and thus earn and experience higher states of consciousness. Because mysticism asks the mystic to model a state of being that they have yet to experience, the enlightenment process becomes arduous and largely unfruitful. In other words, mysticism tries, through cognitive manipulation and behavioral modification, to inhabit an ideal image created by, and in service of, the mind's ego. While its techniques may at times prove partially effective, methods that exclude major parts of self and are fashioned by an unrealized ego become incestuous and lead to fragmented results.

One goal of mysticism is to become loving. But, as we discussed under Devotional Practices, love produced by the mind and ego has nothing to do with essential love. In mysticism practices, the refined form of love imagined by the ego is not derived through an equitable contribution from the feminine, negative polarity. This shoots any effort in the foot; an imagined, intellectual love cannot morph into love that is an essential state of being.

Another goal of mysticism is the humility achieved through devotion to (a positive) spirit. Trying to become humble is a particularly difficult trick, as any recognition of one's own humility also negates it. It takes a fair amount of pride to name humility as a goal in the first place—another effort doomed from the start.

The mystic's striving is a product of ego and can go only so far in the search for truth. Pushing past your emotional nature with the power of mind leaves you conjuring up yet more mental images—images that must remain on this side of the threshold of transcendence. Try making peace with emotions; apply the Emotion Solution steps to mysticism practices and welcome the virtue that stands on its own.

New Age Techniques

Because the majority of new age techniques are geared toward a state of purified, expanded, and enlightened consciousness and bliss, accomplished by ignoring every negative polarity, they do not belong in this list of practices, any more than techniques aimed at destroying all that is positive. The end result of both approaches is identical—the ruin of any possible unity.

Enlightenment Through Body

These methods include enlightenment attained through Eastern yoga practices that use bodily postures, as well as sports and exercise systems in the West. Body paths focus on physicality to the exclusion of chatter from the mind and emotions. This approach is said to lead to an empty and pure state of simple, heightened awareness and vibrant energy flow.

Again, nothing could help these processes more than an open, inquiring stance that includes emotions. While we're often encouraged to somehow buck up during our routines or otherwise overcome teasing mental or emotional intrusions to more or less force our consciousness into a higher state, it's better to simply allow the experience, investigate your responses, and follow them. This approach is how to reach clarity of awareness and simplicity of physical experience quickly and safely. Then your body—along with your thoughts, emotions, and heart—becomes a partner you can work with. It becomes responsive through wholeness of being.

Practicing Presence and Being in the Now (also see Mindfulness)

Being in the present moment is essential to attaining any degree of freedom. But what is amazing is how often being in the moment is confused with practicing a positive attitude. So many people instantly shut out any input they deem "negative," in the name of staying in the present moment. It never seems to cross their minds that the present moment is not something we can control, and that it might contain something other than rays of harmonious light.

Instead, some people turn the goal of being in the moment into a new age whitewashing technique. In pushing negativity outside themselves, they unwittingly create the very thing they are trying to shut out: more negativity. Either they unconsciously act out that negative energy, or if they possess particularly strong nullifying abilities, the energy leaves them entirely and goes out in the world to affect the less fortunate.

The most effective way to ensure against such outcomes is to practice mindfulness that takes in all aspects of our energy unconditionally, whether it's comfortable or not. Then our true nature arrives of its own accord, and presence becomes a matter of course.

Psychological Work

A full and working spirituality cannot be attained to the exclusion of psychology, and vice versa. Many try to create a meaningful life solely through the rigors of psychological investigation, the aim being to develop a strong ego with which to function effectively in the world. Granted, this is an important ability to possess, for a healthy ego is needed to navigate through life. But our ego, in and of itself, can offer only delusive meaning and fulfillment. And left to its own devices, ego does not take kindly to an expanded sense of being, our true nature; it fights spiritual emergence in order to maintain sole command and perspective—as stand-alone psychology lets it do. But by holding the possibility that there may be more to life than the life by and of our ego, we can implement psychological techniques and goals to enhance our spiritual life, while spiritual techniques can greatly enhance our psychological life.

Psychology must make room for more. And psychology does lead to more when we give our emotions full sway, listening to them and remaining open to new possibilities. Ending our investigation at the first sign of psychological relief, however, cuts the process short, for eventually we'll be left wanting, only to be told to look for yet more direction and advice from an ego that speaks only of itself. For integrating psychology with spirituality, the Emotion Solution offers the most direct path.

CHAPTER ELEVEN

Life as Practice, Practice as Life

When we start making strides in owning our discarded energy, the world will become a different place. There'll be no reason to act out, no hidden, dark, swirling energy popping up through ego-driven facades. Stripped of everything that does not support our inborn nature, we'll become free to be exactly who and what we are. And then, running on unadulterated intent, we can offer our unique selves as solid building blocks of society, a structure built through a wholeness that regulates itself, rather than one reflecting errant, cast-aside energy that necessitates ever mounting regulation. While this may sound like a dream in today's world of energetic fracture, we have nowhere else to turn.

A truly unified existence is foreign to us. We have no examples from which to draw, nowhere to look to see what works and give us direction as we strive to create a serviceable culture. We're left with worn paths that are, at best, partially useful. When we look for a model that we can emulate to reach a state of fulfillment, we must do what's always been done: study another's intellectually biased images of personal and social enlightenment, try to embody them through self-discipline and behavioral modification, and then instill them into the populace. But since such deficit-laden efforts haven't worked in the past, there is no reason to think that they'll work in the future. Could the individuals and groups that follow these worn paths thrive once the proper setting and circumstances are available? Possibly. But again, from where does this utopian vision arise? Its architects couldn't help projecting their personal issues and inadequacies onto their plan.

So where do we turn if we want to achieve our collective potential? We must begin where we are: cognizant of the facts that we don't know how to attain such a goal, that previous efforts have not worked, and that we have no viable options. From this starting point, repairing the fractures in the bedrock of our being becomes the obvious next step, and nothing puts right our foundational structure better than embodying the whole of ourselves.

The solution lies in taking back our errant life force, for we forfeit the finer parts of human nature when we close ourselves off from the whole of it, compelling us, both individually and collectively, to use much of our remaining energy to compensate for that loss. We leave ourselves to take part in a frenetic, dog-eat-dog energy grab, either as perpetrators or as victims. Rather than retrieving and living on their own inborn power, the intellectually oriented, many of whom comprise the upper echelons of society, compensate by feeding off the energy of more emotional individuals traditionally relegated to society's lower ranks. And those who are fed upon are left ransacked and must resort to their own unscrupulous devices, compensating for their loss any way they can. On a societal scale, this interplay creates a worldwide lust for energy and resources, acted out on every scale in treachery and wars of acquisition.

While it may be easy to spot a tyrannical neighbor feeding off the energy of her children, or the employer who lords it over his herd, sucking out their life force, we all play the game. Subtly or not, we demand of ourselves and those with whom we interact to behave this way or that, live up to some code, feel and not feel appropriately, not rock the boat, and stick to the norm. We make and keep others smaller, inhibiting them from encompassing the whole of their nature, a whole that would threaten our own stature. Or we reduce ourselves to escape attention and avoid becoming a target. Take note of and sense the dynamics between you and those with whom you associate. There's always an energy exchange, and not always for the better of those involved.

And so it is with our leaders, be they government, corporate, or spiritual, through laws and social norms enacted to clamp down on and bleed the members of an already shunted population. This system guarantees that those at the top of the food chain remain "in charge," with an ample supply of life energy garnered from those on whom they feed. These dynamics can play out only as long as we let them.

We can reverse the tide by taking responsibility for our emotional energy. All else follows. As we're all interconnected, the more of us who own our emotional energy, the more we will positively affect others. With this influence in play, world priorities will change as we become less driven by denied and hidden motives. Look at how much military effort is fear driven and aimed at holding hatred at bay. What will happen when the war-minded recognize their fear and hatred as an internal function and responsibly process it? The same goes for peace enthusiasts, for that matter. Peace proponents and war hawks alike need to deal with their denied hatred, rage, and fear before they can truly become effective. Which group members repress their emotions and which ones act them out is of little significance, for the problems they perpetuate are identical. What common ground these two polarities might find after taking emotional responsibility remains to be seen.

Take yourself back. Look within to the long-abandoned parts of yourself, for what you have thrown aside is what you need to attain a working civilization. A society composed of relatively satisfied, whole, functioning parts is difficult to imagine because it must be realized organically, through the gradual introduction of self-actualized people. This hasn't happened, but by unchaining blocked emotions, we can get there, for doing so reinstates the long-dismissed driver who holds the keys to wholeness of being. But this conversation will remain speculative until we start processing the emotions that open to our greater selves. Do the work to unearth, recognize, and accept your energy, and then allow it to transform into new dimensions and understanding, and it will start to play out societally. This is social responsibility itself.

Postulates

The remainder of this chapter is for those who want to pull out the stops and go for it—those who consciously want to let their energy run free, to be free themselves, and thus to try to unite the divided parts of our fractured world.

What follows is a list of postulates whose objective is to elicit a reaction and get you moving toward wholeness. Most of them will present contrasts to your present assumptions, attitudes, and abilities. In noticing your response to a particular postulate, you can begin the work of embodying that response so that you can go on from there. Whether or not you feel the postulate is true is not the point. Just temporarily entertain it as if it were true, and pay attention to what happens.

For instance, one postulate states, "You are your true nature, and that nature is all-encompassing." Maybe you don't feel that is the case, and you never have. When you consider that postulate, what do you feel *in reaction* that contradicts it? Disappointment? Skepticism? Anger? Sadness? Yearning? Indifference, as if you can't be bothered? Do you feel driven to paste on a sunny disposition and pretend that you consciously realize the whole of your nature? Or do you sense a wall between you and your totality? The idea is that if this postulate sounds good to you but you don't feel that your nature is all-encompassing, the postulate will inevitably bring up the very emotions that are preventing you from consciously merging with your true nature.

Your response may be along the lines of "Yeah, yeah, yeah, I'll give you true nature. You can stick that one where the sun don't shine!" All right! Resentment! Now you're getting somewhere. If you harbor such attitudes, a realized sense of unity with your all-encompassing self is not likely to emerge front and center. But by discovering the etiology of your attitude, by processing what seems to inhibit the realization of your true nature, you gain ground toward that goal. In this way, postulates act as triggers, and triggers simply signal that your emotions demand attention.

If taken to heart, these postulates will not only trigger emotions, but they will also open cracks in your habitual thought forms, constructs, resistances, and defenses. These triggers offer another means to test what might be holding you back from a particular aspect of growth or self-realization. After all, if you actually *are* one with your all-encompassing self, but various issues are preventing you from consciously realizing it, it behooves you to get to know the landscape between you and that achievement. We are all loaded with suppressed, repressed, and denied material that clouds our truth. Putting these postulates into action will help you move into that material.

Another example: To many, the idea of letting emotions take the lead seems counterintuitive, unthinkable, or even heretical because prevailing thought dictates that intellect rules. Of course, this dynamic in itself presents a formidable block to exploring emotional perspectives; if something resides outside your thought and belief systems, there is not much chance you will make an effort to go there. In this case, if you entertain the simple postulate "My emotions can lead the way" and hold it in front of you, in direct contrast to your belief that intellect must lead, some reaction is bound to come up and start you moving. Or not—in which case you can explore your lack of response.

Or say you believe that the best way to create change is through maintaining a positive attitude; any other orientation leads to disaster. After all, constellations of unresolved fear, helplessness, anger, or grief naturally contradict a maintain-a-positive-attitude stance. Not permitting yourself to delve into anything negative might seem beneficial, but how do you know for sure? Maybe what you push away really does have its rhyme and reason. The working postulate here might be "All emotions benefit me, regardless of the good or bad labels I apply to them." Think of this assertion as a possibility and examine it. In doing so, you can uncover specific aversions to accepting the darker shades of your nature, gently explore them, and try making progress.

Some of the following postulates may ring true to you and fall neatly into your present view of reality. Others may not feel relevant to you because their promises do not accord with your belief system. Some may even seem outlandish. That's fine. Whatever a postulate brings up, be it a promise, threat, or snarky laugh, go with it to its destination. No one is asking you to accept a belief without testing contradictory possibilities and proving it for yourself.

Postulate: My true nature is all-encompassing.

Spiritual leaders have proposed variants of this postulate forever. No big news here. Yet few have attained consciousness of this state to the point at which it became their normal, everyday experience. This declaration can shine light on all manner of separation from your true nature.

**Postulate: Since we are all interconnected, I am
connected to and possess all parts of the whole.**

The main point here is that we cannot pick and choose what parts of the whole with which to identify. We are both light and dark, negative and positive, feminine and masculine, good and bad, each of us being composed of all aspects of being. Actually, this is true by reason of contrast: without day, there could not be night, nor could there be negative without the positive; no pole exists without its opposite. This should be obvious, but think of the majority who expunge the negative by reflexively favoring the positive. Serious imbalance, a self-eclipsing existence, results. Start owning everything and follow your reactions.

**Postulate: Favoring one or more energetic pole or
element over another leads to its degradation and
energetic distortion. I now realize everything as equal.**

We've all seen it: the mostly in-the-head person, the emotional wreck, the all-too-sweet soul, the body worshipper who develops few other "muscles," the spiritual adherent who is connected to nothing but their spirit and floats away. The idea here is that respect for all the parts is needed to realize an inclusive, functioning consciousness. And importantly, we have all denied and disparaged our emotional bodies, and this accounts for much of the age-old imbalance on Earth. Imagine giving life to the rest of you, just because the whole is composed of all its parts. What happens?

> **Postulate: Since my mind has controlled my emotions for so long, a temporary emphasis on my emotions will expedite my healing.**

Acting on this postulate presents a dramatic challenge, for it brings our intellect-over-emotion bias front and center. Does the thought of leading with your emotions require a leap of faith? If so, what are you leaping over? What happens if you fall in? If you stand on the other side of the abyss, what does it look and feel like? Judgments against your emotional body are sure to pop up. This postulate also compels you to consider that you harbor a fundamental problem in the first place.

> **Postulate: My emotional energy, especially if denied or repressed, remains energy all the same and retains its power to affect others and me.**

This is a biggie. The law of the conservation of energy states that energy cannot be created or destroyed; it can only be transformed from one form to another. Denying or ignoring an underlying sadness, for example, won't make it disappear or become happiness. In fact your sadness might bleed into the atmosphere while you unconsciously act it out in a damaging manner. Since sadness is an emotion and emotions are energy, your underlying sadness will remain and reappear unless it's processed in your cells and transformed. Keep this postulate in mind so that you can identify instances in which you're not taking responsibility.

**Postulate: My emotions crave acceptance and
continually present themselves for that acceptance.**

Watch the way in which you can't be bothered with your emotions or the degree to which you shove their lessons away. Do you really think rejected emotions don't affect you and others? Whose purpose does it serve to reject them? The emotion is doing its duty, trying to make itself known and move you forward. You might say that the emotion is striving to be seen and accepted as itself, just as most of us would like to be seen and accepted for who we are, rather than having to jump through hoops for acceptance. But more than that, emotions are a power that persists, for discarded emotional energy demands recognition and will create the circumstances in your life that will trigger the emotion over and over until you finally take it in. So in a sense, what you deny is what you create: by pushing away fear, for instance, you create fear-producing situations in your life. This is also true on a collective, global scale. We live in a world whose inhabitants mutually create exactly what we profess not to want, by rejecting those parts of us that would realize our shared dreams. Owning our emotions breaks the cycle.

Postulate: What I have lost can now be found.

Many of us with a particularly strong masculine, intellectual orientation (something that occurs in both men and women) become so far removed from certain emotions that this denied emotional energy leaves our person entirely and takes up residence in people who are not so well defended. There, these cast-off emotions are acted out in ways that seemingly have nothing to do with their original owners, who meanwhile luxuriate within their ivory towers, rolling their eyes at the chaos reigning outside their walls. This energy dumping may seem like a solution, albeit a narcissistic one, but it's no more a solution than cutting off your nose to spite your face. None of us can afford to diminish ourselves. Once rejected, those pieces of self are difficult to retrieve. But even the most heavily defended of us can gain clues to their whereabouts and do the work to reclaim them. If you want to make this your goal, start by paying attention. The signposts are everywhere; simply take the time to notice your emotional reactions to what's happening to the less fortunate around you. With careful attention, you will find that their issues resonate within your own soul. Then do the work to reclaim your energy and free others of your burden.

**Postulate: Nobody has the right to meddle
with the energy of another person.**

On a grand scale, we all submit and are susceptible to each other's emotional orphans. Think of the emotional overlap and poor boundaries between spouses or between children and parents. This situation can be as extreme as one person owning parts of another through coercion, guilt, passive-aggressive behavior, or other types of manipulation. Our emotional baggage gets so mixed in with our personal relationships that distinguishing whose emotion is whose can seem impossible. Only through regaining rejected aspects of yourself can you begin to responsibly disjoin from others and become more whole, doing your part to prevent emotional chaos. Your energy belongs to you and you only. Take rightful possession.

**Postulate: Nobody has the right or the
capability to tell me who I am.**

No one has the blueprint for another's inner being. As the precautionary wisdom states, "If you see the Buddha on the road, kill him." Surrendering to someone else's image of what it is to be whole and functional, either as an individual or in relation to society, may have little to do with your truth.

Postulate: I don't have to do anything I don't want to do.

Take this reactive, defiant stance to its conclusion. This postulate brings you directly back into your formative years and issues. Work through them until you experience the freedom-of-being that resides outside of all constraint.

CONCLUSION

Never before has the power of your true nature been more accessible. Transcendent, problem-solving states of consciousness that took years or even decades to realize through traditional means are now available with predictable ease. The Emotion Solution is a straightforward way to effect these life-changing events, by making peace with, listening to, and embodying the emotions you normally hold at bay—that part of your energetic nature that can finally set you free.

I've shown you the simplicity and advantages of applying this process, and by now I hope you have experienced what it can do. If not, with continued effort and acquired skill, you'll find that your true nature will indeed begin to emerge and, over time, become increasingly accessible. And then, as you persevere, you'll reach critical mass, and your love for truth will become more important than all else. That's cause for celebration because now your process has taken on a life of its own, as cascading realizations allow your true nature to become your predominant identity. Taking energetic responsibility is now ensured for you—it's no longer a question but a staple of your presence. With this internal support, you'll become ever more free and able to inhabit your true self, the stance from which you can make your finest contribution to others.

Nothing affects a person more profoundly than learning to maintain contact with their true nature, yet it remains to be seen how increasing numbers of people who attain such mastery could change society. Nevertheless, I believe therein lies our greatest hope. Just as individuals can reach critical mass, so can societies. When our collective pursuits include taking in and owning all our energy, our society's progress toward a communal wholeness may be inevitable. Becoming your true nature, the whole of who you are, is the greatest gift life has to offer, and it may be the greatest gift you can give to life itself.

ABOUT THE AUTHOR

Fred Carlisle is a licensed certified social worker and gestalt therapist with a master's degree in social work from Smith College. Unsatisfied with available methods of self-development, Carlisle spent decades researching and experimenting with different techniques for emotional healing, which included twelve years of reclusion to face and conquer his personal struggles. He persisted despite discouragement and refused to accept half measures. He emerged from this lengthy process after developing a streamlined practice that addresses mental- and emotional-health issues, dissolves internal barriers to achieving self-development goals, and arrests everyday strife through activating transcendent states of consciousness. Today, Carlisle's greatest ambition is that his discoveries will help readers find permanent solutions to internal conflicts through the power of unreserved emotional acceptance. Visit him at FredCarlisle.com.

CPSIA information can be obtained
at www.ICGtesting.com
Printed in the USA
JSHW052134130920
7839JS00003B/164